THE HENRYS of AKRON

Paternalism and Self-Determination

A Memoir of Childhood, Family, and Career

Don Henry

Printed in the United States of America

First Printing, 2024

Casebound ISBN 979-8-89390-011-8

Perfectbound ISBN 978-8-89390-021-7

DEDICATION

This writing is dedicated to my wife,

Marilyn.

She has made my life an honor to share,

pleasant in every way and a reason to be.

My life has been her life. Her life has been

my life.

INTRODUCTION

I think of my life as hitting an "inside the park" homerun. I touched the bases in life as fast as I could, then doubled back to second base and tagged it again to be certain of my path. Believing I could beat the throw from the outfielder, I rounded third as the Umpire watched. I slid into home hoping the Umpire wouldn't shout, "YOU'RE OUT!"

The journey I've taken began with a handful of seeds stripped from the stalk of a dark green plantain weed growing in Akron, Ohio. An older playmate threw the seeds down my four-year-old throat after promising a surprise. I hacked and coughed. He fooled me. I narrowed my watery eyes, vowed to get even – and not let anyone fool me again. I didn't succeed.

This book isn't about baseball, although some may argue life has always been a hardball game. There are many battlefields to choose. Life's battles are waged by countries, governments, businesses, neighborhoods, families, and in our daily lives. Human nature plays a major role in every contest. Sometimes the stakes are high.

"The Henrys of Akron" looks into the lives of a lower class family as they strive to rise into the middle class. It provides insight for those who have struggled to find financial security that has diminished since World War II. This is a story of why my father and I, later, became job-hoppers and used self-employment as an offensive move when most companies abandoned paternalism. It establishes the element of perseverance as a key ingredient to positive outcomes in facing the unknown.

When you become aware of things in your world during the early stages of life, there are many questions that flash through your mind. Questions about simple things, "No don't use the spoon in that hand, use your right hand." For a time your mind is filled with learning the fundamentals of living and how to get along with people while trying to avoid dangers. It's as if you have become an alien in an unfamiliar world, a hostile place. Although puzzled, you don't ask what your role in this world is; it's too big of a question for an empty mind.

After a few years, you are off to school to learn more about life. Many of life's questions are answered as you are prepared with information to help you gain independence. As you age, your hair begins to fall, wrinkles appear. You wonder about your parents, what they were like when they were young, your ancestors – where they lived, what they looked like, what occupations they had – and you wonder if you possess any of their characteristics, and if they were considered good people.

My story has been extracted from the past. It's a story about family and perseverance, from the mid-twentieth century to the present time with places and events as seen through my eyes. I am a second son born to a father who traveled north from the southernmost tip of Ohio, along the river in Ironton and Coal Grove where he was born. If my Henry grandparents hadn't moved from southern Ohio to Akron around 1930, I wouldn't have been born.

My mother, Eva, was a triplet, born in Wheatland, Pennsylvania, a "Pennsylvania Dutch" and Scottish family background. I was a blonde-haired boy. My brother, sixteen months older, had coal-black hair like my father who was of Irish and Northwest European descent. My brother's difference in coloration and temperament bothered me at times. I was an inquisitive, industrious boy with a penchant for building things and playing with fire. Matches got me into serious trouble, once, when I discovered, "Toilet paper burns real good." I talked a lot and it bothered others. I sensed a need to change which has since been self-corrected, I believe, but I salvaged as much humor as I could out of situations.

I focused on a variety of ways to make money. It started out by collecting pop bottles for deposit, selling sachets door-to-door after clipping out an advertisement in a comic book and built a shoeshine box from a wooden orange crate to set up outside of a beer joint. I got a job selling "Taylor's Home Made Doughnuts" by knocking on doors, became a paper boy for the Niles Daily Times in Niles, Ohio, a bus-boy for a Swedish smorgasbord restaurant where TVs "Cisco Kid," (Duncan Renaldo) stopped in, and then progressed to a regular full-time summer job at a book bindery while in high school. Money and jobs were important and "men have to work," I was taught. My dad was an excellent role model. My mom was a prime example of an excellent wife, mother, and principled woman.

I didn't do drugs or drink alcohol. I didn't do things the easy way. I chose the hard way. It wasn't because I wanted to make things hard, it centers on the decisions made as I traced my path back to second base. Some things I couldn't control. The things I could control, I think, were done in the best interests of my newly formed family and myself. The only way to pay for college during this early period was to sign a regular bank loan, work while attending school, or get an athletic scholarship. What did I do? I did all three.

I was on my way and as I earned college degrees things improved, but human nature entered the picture. I didn't want to continue working for a couple of different companies. There was a strong need to catch up financially, due to seven years of detours, i.e., going back and touching second base. But my primary goal to improve our standard of living never wavered.

I got involved in "job-hopping" resulting from bottom-line problems for some companies, and reaching for my own goals in other situations.

As I headed for home plate my journey resulted in establishing a chain of retail stores my wife and I founded – neither of us had any experience in retail management, whatsoever. It worked well for ten years. Sales declined and mall stores began to think about closing their doors. In 1987, we sent out resumes with fingers crossed due to my sketchy wild and wooly industrial and retail work history. Fortunately, less than a year later I hired into a stable company in Cincinnati that had U.S. and international manufacturing locations in the U.K. and Japan. It provided a solid seven years of industrial experience and I was promoted to Vice President. The good times ended when the company changed direction. It sold out. We were cannibalized.

What to do, what to do?

I picked up the phone book and, again, starting from scratch, I established a completely new business. It was 1995. My income exploded!

By now, I had no fear of anything. I experienced about everything I could think of, imagine, or envision with regard to companies, bosses, colleagues, and working for a living – except for starvation. So bring it on. Starvation wouldn't be so bad, or would it? I'd experienced that before. So, bring it on, anyway.

What's going to happen? Up until now, everything has turned out okay.

The Henrys of Akron

1940 to 1947

"Shut your eyes, and open your mouth," my friend said. "I've got a surprise." I shouldn't have done it. I was four years old, trusting and gullible enough to think something good would be offered. It wasn't Christmas. The summer sun beat down on my straw-blonde hair, causing my blue eyes to squint – his dark eyes were devilishly bright.

We were playing "war," the Japs and the Germans, in a lot behind the Spicer Theater on East Exchange Street in East Akron. It was 1944, August, enough time for the dark green plantain weed in northeast Ohio to produce a single stalk, loaded down with seeds at its tip. The weed looks like a miniature cattail. Its seeds can be easily stripped off the stalk by grabbing the seed and pulling the stalk between your thumb and first finger, leaving a pile of seeds in your hand.

I've forgotten the name of my playmate, but he must have been six or seven years old and wiser than I in the ways of human nature. He promptly heaved a handful of seeds down my throat. I was shocked. I remember the panic, choking, and bitter taste as I ingested the seeds, drawing in air and sucking them further into my windpipe. Through the hacking, gasping and short-fingered effort to dislodge the seeds, I heard squeals of laughter. Hilarity consumed my playmate. He bent over with laughter. I struggled to dislodge the seeds and get air into my lungs.

He put one over on me. My watering eyes narrowed, I vowed to get even – and not let anyone fool me again. I didn't succeed.

I was born on June 9, 1940. The day after my birth, President Franklin Roosevelt addressed the country about the war in Europe. He told the country Mussolini had joined with Hitler to declare war on France, "On this the tenth day of June, 1940, the hand that held the dagger has struck it into the back of its neighbor."

Our family lived with my maternal grandmother at the time, Grandma Nettie Erwin. She was blind. I don't think she had enough time for sympathy nor ever wanted it, after having raised four children and giving birth to triplets – my mother being one, but losing one at birth – and living with an alcoholic husband, Grandpa Tom Erwin. Apparently, he wouldn't work a regular job. He left the family at some point, leaving Grandma to fare for herself. The first time I remember seeing Grandpa, he was living at a "workhouse" in western Pennsylvania, near Sharon. He lifted me up and held me close, face-to-face, under his wide-brimmed dark brown hat; white hair whisked out from underneath his hat. I must have been about three years old at the time – I immediately liked him, and don't know why.

It seemed strange still in my younger years sending someone to a workhouse who wouldn't work. I found out later on it was a county home, not a workhouse; somehow I had gotten that part of Grandpa's story wrong. My Uncle Kenny Erwin and my brother corrected me. I saw him only one other time during a visit to our home in Akron in 1948, taking a break from the "home," and have a picture of him sitting on our back porch smoking a corncob pipe. The other time I thought about him, Mom was talking to Grandma by telephone. Tears came into Mom's eyes. Grandpa had wandered away from the county home at night in the middle of winter. He was found in a nearby field the next day by a hunter. He had died. I think Mom said he was senile and got lost; today I wonder about Alzheimer's.

Grandma & Grandpa Erwin

We lived in a twinplex Grandma rented. I don't know if twinplex was a word used in the forties or if someone made it up in our family, don't remember, but that was its design. It was an old, wood-sided house, gray in color, with a front porch split in two by a wooden railing, and two front doors identifying it as a two family, accommodating another family on the other side. The house had a total of two floors plus an attic and featured a slate roof. The Mitchell family, Mildred and John, lived on the other side with five kids. There were five of us on our side: Mom, Dad, my brother Bob, Grandma and me. My brother was sixteen months older, born February 10, 1939. The only name I knew for my brother, for the most part was "Brother." We had the same name it seemed – he called me brother also, and that's what the family used when referring to us, "Give it to brother. Go with brother." Outsiders would laugh at the two of us, but it didn't matter. We still called each other brother, never by our given names. It wasn't until nearly high school we mutually dropped the brother usage. Then, "Bobby" sounded like I was referring to a stranger every time I said his name. It took a while to get used to the simple, but necessary change.

Grandma memorized locations of obstacles in the rooms, whether a chair, floor lamp, or table. She never used a cane, although she had a red-tipped, white wooden cane used by blind people. When she left the house, a friendly arm guided her. She peeled potatoes, and apples to make pies from scratch, and cooked the best rice pudding I'd ever tasted. She cleaned house and did almost everything a sighted person could do. She amazed me. I never knew her to lose a sense of humor about most things. It seemed to me she was embarrassed about her handicap. The problem began with sunstroke at two years of age, my mom told me, and at seventeen she was legally blind. Her maiden name was Gentholtz, "Pennsylvania Dutch," and she traveled in Pennsylvania, near Wheatland and Sharon. If blindness wasn't enough, she also suffered from large weeping ulcers on front of her lower left leg, requiring daily cleansing and wrapping. Grandma Erwin would "watch" us when Mom and Dad were working.

In an upstairs bedroom closet, Brother and I rummaged through Grandpa's World War I items. The stowed gear included a helmet, uniform, rifle, a bayonet, and most intriguing – a gas mask, charcoal canister, straps and all. When we were caught in the closet by someone, one of us would be wearing the dangling oversized gas mask trying to out-scare the other one. It looked skull-like with big insect eye ports and a leather or canvas material with a tan colored, smelly face. Old things always seem to have a musty smell about them.

The house was situated behind storefront buildings, with apartments above and around back, beside the cement block Spicer Theater. Behind the theater was a weed filled lot with a partially demolished building. We were cloistered on all sides by buildings, and played in the short dirt yard and driveway to the side of our house that separated the structures. On occasion we'd go into Islay's Dairy around front for a thick "shake," and down Exchange Street to the corner of Spicer Street where the trolley tracks intersected at People's Drugstore, complete with wooden phone booths and soda fountain. I had my first run-in with the law at the drugstore.

My mother had taken me into People's on one of her visits. As she got busy locating her needs, my attention focused on a Whiz candy bar that looked interesting, then a pack of bubble gum. I must have had pockets in my coat. She wasn't aware of my shopping until we got home. I don't think I knew the difference between wanting something and the need to exchange something. I was aware of "red cents" and a stamp with a picture of a cannon on it. I think these were used for exchanges, but I'm not clear whether I knew anything about money at the time. You just walked into a store and took whatever you wanted from the shelves. That's what everyone did in the store, my mom included. Money must have been a secret thing, something most people didn't have. I didn't see much of it that I remember. It was a good life while it lasted.

When we got back home, I pulled out the candy bar. It didn't take Mom long to spot it. I don't

Mom - Eva Lena Henry

think I'd even begun to unwrap it yet, when she demanded, "Where did you get that?"

In an abrupt about face, I didn't even have my coat off – she marched me down Exchange Street in front of Islay's and turned the corner into People's. On the way without much discussion, she admonished me, "You can't take something that doesn't belong to you. You have to take the candy back and tell him you're sorry." She seemed angry, by the way she yanked me along with her at a fast pace.

She held me by the coat collar and took me up to the man behind the counter. He leaned over the counter to look into my eyes. He must have seen this kind of thing before, with me on my toes and my mom in firm control of my movements. I looked at the floor.

"How can I help you?" he asked, smiling.

"Tell him what happened and apologize. Say you're sorry." I didn't know what apologize meant, I hadn't done much of that up to this point, but I knew what sorry meant. I peered up at the man and did as I was told.

"I'm sorry for taking your candy."

The storeowner was nicer than my mom. He smiled brightly in a funny way. I was pretty confused. My mom was mad as hell. The guy who should have been mad at me was nice as hell. After giving him the bubble gum and Whiz, he handed me a sucker. But, it was taken gently from my hand, with Mom saying, "No, thank you. He has to learn a lesson." From then on, when I went into People's store, the man smiled at me as I turned out my pockets to show him I understood the law regarding candy shopping. Mom always taught us simple truths of growing up. She was a great mom.

Mom didn't go past the seventh grade, and my dad, the ninth. That's the way life happens when both sides of the family have fathers who drink for a living and work for the money they drink. They pawn household appliances when they don't work; the wives and kids have to pick up the difference if they are able. That's what my mom and dad did – they worked. They grew up with alcohol affecting their lives and became determined to do better, and to keep us away from exposure to the main problem that had made their lives difficult and unbearable. Except for a brown-bagged bottle – one found behind Grandma's in the

Grandma & Grandpa Henry

alley running behind her house, a little blackberry wine left in the bottle that tasted real sweet on a hot summer day – I hardly touched the stuff.

My dad was either two or three years older than my mother. The reason for the uncertainty occurred later in his life when he was diagnosed with terminal cancer. In getting his papers in order, it became apparent there was a mix-up along the way. An original birth certificate had to be obtained from Union Furnace, Ohio, where he was born. The certificate didn't match the date his mother had established for his birthday by one year. All this time he had been under the impression he was older. Instantly, he lost a year of age. Unfortunately it wasn't good news that caused the discovery.

Dad was from a family of six kids, all boys except for Maxine. His age must have been unimportant to his mother, Maggie. Between Grandpa Henry's binges, trips to the pawnshop to get her goods back, her work as a cleaning lady and nurse's aide, Dad's birth year must have gotten lost in the shuffle. His father, Arthur, didn't involve himself in such matters. But, my dad always had a soft spot for his father in spite of the problems he caused. He told me about taking lunch to Grandpa Henry where he worked as a mason, when the Quaker Oats silos were being built in Akron. In the early 1980s, the grain silos were converted into hotel rooms inside the silos and the business was called Quaker Square, near The University of Akron.

My dad was double-promoted from seventh grade to ninth grade, but had to drop out of school to help his mother with the family fortune. He hardly ever drank, although there are a couple of occasions that stand out. He worked hard and yet suffered hard times for most of his life due to a variety of circumstances, none of them having anything to do with alcohol.

The war wasn't discussed much with me – what could a five-year-old contribute to the calamity that began December 7, 1941, and destroyed hundreds of thousands of lives?

"We're going to turn out the lights now and lie on the floor," my mother said.

"What for?" asked I.

"It's a blackout," she said.

"Why?"

"In case of an air attack, an air raid, the planes won't see our lights."

"What's an air raid?" again, I asked.

"Donny, be quiet. It'll only be a little while." She comforted me, with an arm tightly wrapped around me and my brother.

I hugged the rough, red wool-like carpet. It scratched my face – musty, dusty and black in the eerie sightless silence. Silence, the only difference to Grandma Erwin sitting in a chair quietly save for her thoughts of World War I when she was in her mid-twenties, with two children at the time, and Grandpa Erwin was stationed in the Army.

The Japs in the Pacific and the Germans in Europe, I found out, were the enemies. I added a new word to my growing vocabulary. Enemy – someone you dislike bad enough to kill, and someone who hates you bad enough to kill you.

"Why?" I asked.

By now we were sneaking into the Spicer Theater on a semi-regular basis. We waited until the cashier in her little boxed window booth sold all of the tickets before the show started and left the box. Ducking low past the booth with swiftly churning little duck legs, a pack of us would steal away into the darkness, down the aisle of the sloped seating. We were treated to many adventure movies – brother and our gang – watching enemies die in newsreels and seeing the enemy atrocities they committed before dying themselves. It seemed fair they should die and we should win. I learned about politics in black and white at no cost to my parents, made wooden guns, and killed Japs and Germans in the abandon half-demolished building behind the Spicer Theater. I always got killed. I had to be a German.

Sometimes we paid a dime for the show, or maybe a nickel, after collecting pop bottles for deposit. Most of the time we didn't pay. The only time we became fearful of being caught, happened when the lights were turned on in-between features to collect for the March of Dimes fight against polio. We imagined ushers could remember everyone who paid to get in, and we, therefore, would stand out like several yellow jellybeans in a jar filled with bright green ones.

The only other foreboding feeling at the Spicer occurred during a newsreel, "Movie Tone News," covering the death of President Franklin Roosevelt. The long procession, the hollow pounding drumbeat, the caisson drawn by six large white clip-clop horses, with a black drape over the coffin and the somberness of it all scared me. This was the only movie I remember clearly at the Spicer during that period of time – pictures from April, 14, 1945. President Roosevelt was buried the next day.

My dad walked into the kitchen at Grandma's fresh from outside. He was wearing a lightweight plain beige jacket. "It doesn't look good," he said.

"No, Vern! No!" Mom's voice quivered, tightened and whined at once.

"I might have to go," he said.

She clung to him. My brother and I stood motionless. What did he mean? Why was Mom so upset?

Dad - Arthur Vernon Henry

"They've scheduled a physical. We'll have to wait and see how things go. It must not be getting better, after all," he said.

She hugged him and wouldn't let him go.

Brother whispered, "It's the Japs."

As it turned out, Dad never had to leave for the war effort. He had gotten a physical, but the exact timing is lost. It had to have been by mid-1945 because the fortune of the war changed when a decision to drop the world's most powerful bomb got a green light. At the time he drove a big rig tractor and trailer for Red Star Trucking Company, headquartered in Akron, Ohio.

Before meeting Eva, my mother, he worked in Ironton as a boy loading boxcars with terra-cotta sewer pipe. He learned how to drive a truck before his family moved to Akron. After moving north about 1930, he worked in the mill room at Goodyear Tire and Rubber Company. The mill room didn't allow him to see the light of day which he grew to dislike. It wasn't long before he took to the open road as a truck driver. He drove truck until he retired from work due to his health.

An odd thing happened at Grandma's house, actually on top of the house. It involved one of Dad's younger brothers. This brother was about thirteen years old and theatrically inclined. At about ten o'clock in the morning, one of the Mitchells rushed up to our front door and said Dad's brother was on the roof threatening to jump. Well, that started a commotion in the neighborhood and ruined the morning calm. We ran outside and sure enough my uncle was straddling a peak high up on the slate roof. Anyone familiar with slate knows how slippery the surface can be, especially if it's a little damp.

"I'm going to jump. Get away," he yelled. His eyes were large and scary. You could see his eyes from the front yard where I was standing. He appeared to mean business. Otherwise, he seemed unemotional about the prospect of flattening himself on the driveway beside the house.

This would-be thespian succeeded in gaining an audience with the Mitchells and the people who came out of their apartments surrounding Grandma's house. They gathered around to watch what would happen to the crazy kid in the limelight on a precarious slate roof stage. After more hollering up, the hollering response down, and coaxing him to get hold of his senses, a huge bright red hook and ladder fire truck arrived. Its siren turned off with its orange beacon flashing, the truck eased between the Spicer Theater and apartment buildings, down the narrow driveway running beside Grandma's house.

Up close, this was great theater. The firemen jumped out of the truck and began questioning my mom and dad. Then they fixed their eyes on the kid on top of the roof with their own line of questions.

"Hey, what are you doing up there?" one shouted into the bullhorn.

"Come on down, before you hurt yourself," admonished another.

This artful exchange only encouraged my uncle to climb to the highest and uppermost peak of the twinplex, some thirty feet high.

"Look out, I'm going to jump," he shouted.

The firemen deployed a twelve-foot net under the peak where he was perched. They each took a position around the net stretching it. There were about six or seven of them in full gear, with yellow slickers and fire helmets, their fire station number larger than any other legible wording on the helmets.

"If you're going to jump, jump into the netting," one instructed over a bullhorn. "Come on, let's get this over with. Jump, we'll catch you."

He must have had a Superman complex, unconcerned about the height. If he was acting, he was doing a good job. As I stood there watching the performance by act and scene, he became a symbol of courage and stupidity rolled into a personage I felt slightly embarrassed to know. But, I still had to call him, Uncle, and it couldn't be avoided – he was my dad's brother. On the other side of things, it was exciting and free entertainment.

Since he wasn't going to come down on his own, in the same manner he ascended the stage, or jump, they decided to go up after him. The buildings were too close to utilize the ladder so two firemen entered the house and climbed to the second floor. They exited a bathroom window at the rear of the house, the shortest route to the teenage entertainer. With some resistance they finally subdued and dragged my uncle through the bathroom window. He was still wild-eyed as they led him out through the audience into an ambulance. He hosted an after-the-show crowd waiting for him to arrive at the local city hospital, consisting of nurses and a doctor or two. My uncle's weird performance lasted for three hours and has remained a puzzle ever since. No explanation was given or discussed from that time to this. Given the status of his family life it shouldn't have been surprising, nor his subsequent move to Hollywood, California, years later where he sought fame and established an unconventional lifestyle.

The Japanese part of the war ended quietly at my Grandma's house, after the Atomic Bomb dropped-in on Hiroshima on August 6, 1945, and three days later on Nagasaki August 9, 1945.

I was the youngest among the "Spicer Gang," as we became known. We didn't have guns or weapons, not even bean shooters – ragged pants and worn tennis shoes became our typical, local uniforms. We managed to get caught a few times sneaking into the theater. At least, I had company as another forced march down the driveway and out front to the Spicer ensued. This time Mom had both, my brother and me in tow. When the gang started school, I was left behind. I convinced my mom to let me wait at the corner of Spicer Street and the alley for the kids to come home from school. I sat on the sidewalk under a tree watching black carpenter ants bump into each other and stared at the street running up the hill to Mason Elementary for signs of life – like women in New England who stood on their Widow's Perch longing for their seafarer's return from the sea. I wanted to go to school, too.

Prior to entering first grade, the idea seemed adventurous and much sought after. I don't remember kindergarten or if it was available before 1946. Maybe not. There had been a teacher shortage during the war as teachers joined the war effort to work in factories across the United States. Finally, it was my turn.

In preparation for the event, Mom took time off from her job as a check-out cashier at the local Kroger Grocery to get some medicine. She wanted me to go with her. We stepped off of a bus and walked a block, entering a huge red brick building. As we approached our destination halfway down the hallway, I heard kids screaming. I asked, "Why?" I soon found out as a vaccination was underway. They rolled up my sleeve. Stab, stab, stab, the flat faced half-inch round needle never stopped. Red-faced with pain, I came close to crying, but didn't. I was growing up, and "Grownups don't cry," my mom said. I think she said that for her own benefit, not mine, because she couldn't bear to see her kids hurt.

My grown-up day arrived. I entered first grade at Mason Elementary in September, 1946, while still living at Grandma Erwin's. My mother walked up the celebrated hill with me and turned over her youngest son to another's care amid terrified screams, disorganization, and mothers' pleas for their kids to settle down. I raised my eyebrows as my mom closed the door. I wondered what had I gotten into. Staring at black ants on the sidewalk had benefits – no screaming terror, at least. I waited for this?

A few months before we left the comfort of Grandma's for good, my brother and I had developed an intense interest in marbles. It was a rite of passage into older kids' circles. Since we were beginners and hadn't developed the skill to compete with more experienced kids, our "bombs" and "sticks" were off target – we lost more than we won. We guarded a dwindling supply of the multi-colored glass marbles as measured by the small diameter of the "marble socks" where we stored them. After school one day my brother and I came upon a "high-roller." He had more marbles than he needed, apparently, because he was jumping up and down on top of a flat roof over the front porch at the corner of Spicer Street and the alley. He tossed marbles into the eager hands fighting over them on the sidewalk below. We joined into the fray for a free share of the marbles.

Steelees, purees, solids and other orbs were flying and bouncing all around us like manna from heaven. The more agitated and aggressive we beggars became, the more enjoyment the "roller" exhibited. The free-for-all didn't erupt into an altercation; it seemed inevitable, but not long after we joined-in my bother dashed between two parked cars to chase a puree and got hit by a car coming down Spicer from the direction of People's.

He bounced off of the gray car's right front fender and hit the pavement. I thought he might be dead. The guy driving braked, but couldn't stop in time. The driver jumped out. My brother pulled himself up on one arm. He looked dazed, but got up. The shaken driver helped him up and asked where he hurt, and where he lived.

"I don't have a home," said my brother, kicking and struggling to break free from the man's grasp.

The driver was dismayed. The boy he had just hit ran from him and disappeared between two buildings. The group that chased marbles, now took off after my brother and chased him. When we caught up with him someone asked, "Why'd you run?" His blue jeans were torn at the knees and you could see a scrape and blood running down one leg.

"I don't want my mom to know. I'll get a whippin'," he said.

Don and Bob

My brother was a tough kid. He limped a little, but became a local hero to most of us. First for being so tough, and second for not wanting to tell his mom. He told me not to say anything and I promised. He was my brother, a hero, and he'd be a hero again, a real one, but again no one would know.

In the summer of 1946, my dad bought a lot to build a house. A baby girl was on the way and would be born March 16, 1947, a day before St. Patrick's Day. Since my dad claimed Irish descent he named her Patricia. The claim as far as I knew seemed legitimate based on Grandpa Henry's disposition for drinking and fighting, but any claim to missionary zeal was not. Her name was inspired by an American revolutionary orator, Patrick Henry of Virginia. Grandpa's people trekked up the Ohio Valley from Virginia through Kentucky. Rather than trace that tree and be found wrong, the romanticism of being related to an original patriot is still possible. It has been left unattended, so we aren't left overly disappointed.

The lot my dad bought was small, located in an area on the outskirts of Akron in Springfield Township, at the end of a dead-end yellow dirt and gravel road. We were city kids, used to adventurous lives filled with old abandoned, broken down buildings and busy city streets. The lot bordered a dense wooded area and, indeed, the lot was carved out of the woods.

The House Dad Built

We ran through the darkened woods with no fear, no bearings or any street names to guide us.

We watched Dad swing the hatchet and axe to clear a small area then place cement blocks on a patch of clearing that became the foundation for the house he was determined to build. The blocks were set on the side, three blocks high. A truck delivered the two-by-fours and two-by-six dimensional lumber; his hammer swung and the ding of the force drove the spikes home. He allowed me to help him hammer nails since I had some experience. I used a hammer for the first time at Grandma's on the steps going upstairs to the bedrooms. I got yanked out of the darkened stairway after sinking a few nails, at random, into the wooden steps.

It wasn't surprising at the time Dad would set out to build a house. It wasn't done in the traditional way with blueprints and helpers. He was the only one working, no carpenters, electricians, or plumbers – no one else showed up. Actually, we didn't need plumbers, a hole was dug with a rectangular box set on top of a large square hole in the ground that added to my vocabulary – outhouse. For water, I learned you could call someone who would show up with a drilling rig and before you knew it, the driller proclaimed, "Water!" A hand pump was installed on top of the small hole the driller bored near the foundation of the house. We didn't need plumbing because nothing was in the house, everything was outdoors. The house measured about ten feet wide by twenty feet long with an attached bedroom in back, eight by ten feet long finished inside with a living room and kitchen where the one and only door in the house was located. It was all ours. My brother and I slept in the living room on fold-up cots.

We were happy, if not rich. We had our very own home and nobody lived on the other side, only the fresh air and trees, and the animals that popped out of the woods. The new home offered an adventure in country living mid-forties style with cold running well water, a pot-belly stove, the latest accommodations for personal needs, no bathtub except for a three foot metal circular zinc-coated tub, and a brand new outhouse that included wild bird serenades piercing the cracks of the wooden structure. I spent a lot of time in the tub; it was easy-in and easy-out without the slightest slippage.

It didn't take long for my brother and me to adapt to this new way of living. We ran around the sparsely settled neighborhood, free to go anywhere, bare feet, no shirts and a rope to hold up our britches. We got into as much mischief as we could find. The local inhabitants seemed unhappy and irritated at our presence; the blue jays squawked, crows swooped at us, rabbits and gray squirrels quickly high-tailed away in an opposite direction, and the sunfish and bluegill dove deep when we showed up above the clear water. Later when we appeared with sling shots, bow and arrow, and a tree branch with knotted butcher string terminating in a safety-pin hook, it revealed our intentions and caused a higher level of anxiety throughout the woods. Our conversion from city life to the back woods of Springfield Township required no training, it fit our natural inclination to adapt and change to whatever requirement the situation demanded. We only had to help out when asked, or when we sensed our mom needed assistance.

Too soon the new school year started. I entered second grade at Roosevelt Elementary. For the first time we were picked up by a yellow school bus and transported to school. We walked about a half-mile from 37 Meadowridge Road to the entrance of our dead-end street at Albrecht Avenue. We spent a lot of time at the corner waiting for the bus shivering in winter. I thought it would have been better to keep walking and fend off the cold, rather than wait, but once inside the school after doffing our coats in the cloakroom, we warmed up fast.

I was quite a talker at the time. In-between spelling, multiplication tables and reading, I must have been talking to someone. Then our report cards came out. I carried it home to my mother in an envelope. I guess the content was confidential and a plain brown wrapper, appropriate. A parent had to sign the back of the card signifying a careful reading had taken place, but in reality to guarantee the parent had received the card. Well, it worked.

"Donny Ray, what do you have to say about this?" Mom asked.

I feigned surprise and thought there was some humor in the "F" I had worked several weeks to achieve. "Why?" I asked laughing. I was a talkative, humorous little boy up to this time.

"You wait 'till your dad gets home. You won't think it's funny when he sees this. You aren't going to fail!"

Uh-oh! Well, I stopped laughing. This was serious. Mom was the law, but Dad was the enforcer. Up until now I thought they both liked me, but now I wasn't sure. Mom meant business. I longed for the carpenter ants on the sidewalk at Grandma's. School was losing favor in my mind. All it did was get me into trouble with the teacher, and now my mom and dad. I knew whatever was in store for me, it wasn't good. Even with an F, a failing grade, I was smart enough to know that.

Mom huddled with Dad when he got home from work. He yanked me out of a comic book, and asked,

"Do you have anything to say about this F?"

"No," I muttered, trembling.

"Your teacher says you are always talking and not paying attention. You will, and you won't think it's funny to get Fs!" he scolded. Abruptly, he unstrapped his belt. He whacked me several times. It stung. I didn't cry. I had to hold my breath with each lash, but I didn't cry.

It may have been the first time I got the belt instead of a hand spanking. Maybe not, but it's the first time I remember. There would be others.

As a result of the home schooling with Dad's belt, education and especially grades rose in value. They became synonymous with well-being and the difference between life and death. Talking declined significantly in worth. I began to lose my sense of humor, laughing at things carefully and never received another failing grade. If there was a lesson in it, I owe it to my mom for raising the issue, and to my dad for caring so much, and to his belt, which I gazed at with more respect on occasion. Maybe my dad had a bad day and was tired; maybe – he was just hungry.

During the first winter in the house on Meadowridge Road, two memories stand out. The first one concerns the Christmas tree in the living room my brother and I slept beside, waiting for Santa Claus. By day there were stuffed chairs to sit in and at night we rolled out the cots. It had been speculated at school that Santa didn't exist. On this night we got confirmation. I became determined to find out if the old guy was real or not. With my right eye half-closed about to surrender to sleep, out of the darkness my mom and dad crept, placing presents under the tree. When finished, they crept back into their room thinking they had gotten away with the good deed. I didn't let on, but I woke my brother and whispered to him what I saw. We kept it quiet, not knowing if Santa might end if we didn't play dead about it. Obviously, our parents didn't have money and caused me to think we were getting toys when it was hard to find money for milk at times. Yet, they let Santa get all of the credit. I wondered how many other parents were doing the same thing. I felt sad about these kind of things happening for holidays and birthdays and began to think everyone should get paid the same amount of money, as my mom has said many times, "No one is any better than anyone else."

A bad situation developed one night when Dad came home from an apparent drinking episode. Most of the time we didn't have a car; of necessity he walked down Meadowridge Road to catch a ride to Red Star where he worked and drove a semi. He purchased a fifteen year old 1931 Ford Model A rumble seat coupe, before winter set in. The car ran out of gas close to home. It was snowing. Financial pressures and a growing family, or perhaps depression may have been at work on his mind. I don't know. He wasn't far inside the door when Mom let out a tirade of derision. It left no doubt she wouldn't have alcohol in the family and around her kids. Dad was docile at first. Soon enough they were raising their voices.

Dad was not given to long dialogue. He grabbed a wooden chair and heaved it through the only window in the living room, shouting, "I work, and work, and work and this is what I get when I come home?"

Mom screamed back at him. He glared and walked out of the door in the kitchen. The thin curtains blew through the opening where there once was a window. Some snowflakes drifted inside, across a lamp, and settled wet on the linoleum floor. Wide-eyed and shivering, my brother and I consoled Mom by saying, "Dad will be back." We didn't know of course, if he would or not. It looked serious. We hadn't ever seen him act like this before. She pulled our nightshirts down and hurried us off to her room, tucking us into her bed to get us out of the drafty cold invading the living room.

A while later the chug-chug of the Model A approached our driveway. I stood in the bedroom doorway listening and watching the kitchen door. A sheepishly, shivering father entered. He hugged Mom. He didn't say anything. It was all right again. Dad set to work tearing open some cardboard boxes he'd gotten somewhere and taped them together to cover the window. When he was done, he looked at Mom, my brother, and me. He looked at each of us, individually.

"I'm sorry, Eva. I'm sorry, kids."

We knew he meant it.

For Valentine's Day in 1947, the grade school classes at Roosevelt made red hearts from construction paper for their mothers. I took special care to make the best one I could. Since both my brother and I had artistic ability from Dad, my confidence in making the best heart in second grade wasn't unrealistic. I cut carefully, pasted with dexterity, and added the lace fringe perfectly to its border. The printing was the best I could muster – "I love you, Mom," – and much better than any writing exercise I'd done for the teacher. I took my time. When the heart was finished I sat back with pride and couldn't wait to get home to give it to Mom.

We got off of the bus at the corner of Albrecht and Meadowridge. All of the kids had hearts in their hands walking down the graveled, muddy road on their way home. The snow melted making everything sloppy. I kept eyeing my brother's valentine and thought mine was better. Halfway home a gust of wind snatched my heart and whisked it ten feet ahead dashing it into a ditch beside the road filled with muddy water. I ran after it as quickly as I could, but when I lifted the red heart from the ditch, the muddy stain ruined the valentine. Rather than giving her a dirty, wet, and spoiled card, I threw it back into the ditch and cursed the wind.

My brother handed his heart to Mom. She ran her hands over it, kissed him, and said it was beautiful. Mine was better.

"Donny, do you have one too?"

"No," I said, shaking my head. Thinking it would be better to have her think that than to say it got ruined and thrown away - I just said, no.

"I saw the kids coming home. They all had valentines for their mothers. Didn't you make one for me?" A glaze gave way to some slight tearing in her eyes.

Seeing she was hurt, I said, "I threw it away." Before I could say anything else, she started to cry. "Mom, Mom. It wasn't good enough. It got all wet and muddy. It was really good, but I didn't want you to have a bad one."

She stopped tearing. A bright smile replaced the hurt she had felt. "Is that what really happened?"

"Yes, honest, Mom. That's what happened. Isn't it Brother?"

My brother nodded his head in agreement.

Everything was okay, again. I could always count on my brother. If it had to do with big kids giving me trouble or other kinds of problems, he was always there to jump in to help me. He always gave me a hand. We fought as most brothers do, but not seriously.

Maybe I shouldn't have been so sure I could outdo my brother's effort and make a better valentine than he had made. Maybe I should have gripped the valentine with more strength and been alert to the gusts of high wind. Maybe I should have put it under my coat. Maybe that's what they mean when they say there is, "pride before the fall."

I wasted all the time and effort I spent attempting to make a perfect valentine. I also made my mom cry, and now the valentine was face down, drowning in a ditch filled with muddy water because I couldn't hold on.

Maybe, maybe …

1947 to 1949

In March the new baby arrived. Much to the pleasure of both Mom and Dad, it was a pink occasion, a baby girl. Patricia was blonde and blue-eyed. At least she wasn't a boy. We would have had trouble with names like Brother, Brother, and Brother.

Either Mom got tired of the difficult living conditions – having to heat water on the electric stove for washing clothes, dishes, baths, and rushing back and forth to the outhouse, especially in the winter and foul weather, hauling coal and water in from outside when we weren't there to help – or else Dad's new job at Zeno Brothers Trucking Company gave him enough of an increase in his paycheck to make a move to a better house with better living conditions.

In April, 1947, the small house passed on to a new owner. The sale of the small structure on Meadowridge became a signal for new beginnings and four good years for the Henrys. The new house seemed like a large mansion after living in the one floor, ten foot by twenty foot house by the woods. This was a two story house about sixteen hundred square feet of living space with a finished third floor attic, a basement, hot and cold water, three regular bedrooms and a real bathroom with a real bathtub. We had a small front yard with grass and a deep backyard with fruit trees ending at the alley. The fruit trees consisted of sour cherry, plum, pear and quince. Quince … "What's a quince?" I asked.

We moved our wooden metal-lined icebox with us to 429 Talbot Avenue. Some people on Talbot owned an electric refrigerator with ice cubes. We placed a printed cardboard sign in the window; on one side in blue letters was the word, "ICE", on the other side in red letters, "NO ICE". The iceman driving by in a truck would stop if he saw the blue side in the window on our front porch. He'd select a block of ice about sixteen inches square, then using large tongs he'd penetrate both sides of the ice, heft it to his leather padded shoulder, carry it into the house and deposit it into the ice chest. He'd collect twenty-five cents and be on his way down the street. The process took long enough for us to swish through the long shards of ice in the bottom of the truck and grab a clear, unflavored chunk of ice. Even harder to believe, now, we had a milkman deliver milk to our door, a ragman in a horse drawn wagon, who shouted from the street, "Rags – any rags today?" A fruitman in a horse drawn wagon carrying a variety of fruit who shouted, "Bananas, get your bananas here," much like the way peanuts are sold at baseball games. All of the relics of the forties traveled down Talbot Avenue. We got there as they were about to disappear from the face of the earth.

Mom and Patty

Mom was extremely happy with her new home. I'm sure Dad got a lot of satisfaction from the sale of the house he built. They were happier than I'd ever remembered. But good times never seem to last nearly long enough. What's comes next is anyone's guess.

The new street had sidewalks lined with poplar trees, maple and other species up and down the street. The surface of Talbot was made of red brick end-to-end, said to have been laid during the WPA funding as a result of the Great Depression. Our street paralleled Arlington Street to the east, with a black cinder alley between the two streets. The closest intersection was five houses to the north at the base of Fifth Avenue hill, the site of Zickafoose's market. The houses were tightly packed together with driveways on each side, and no more than two feet to spare on each side of the driveway next to the houses. They looked like row houses with a variety of construction styles in this upper-lower class neighborhood. Most of the men worked in rubber factories in Akron; Goodyear, Firestone, B.F. Goodrich, General Tire and assorted industries throughout the Akron area.

The new found prosperity was great, but we were still without a car. The old Model A had lost its engine. Zeno's permitted Dad to take the orange colored tractor home, a White

Dad & White Motors tractor

Motors model, and use it as transportation when his "run" was completed. The new job was long distance driving, whereas Red Star was more local. He was gone a lot more because of "layovers" when a load wasn't ready for a return trip, or the distance too great to return in a day's time. That meant he wasn't home a lot of nights. I appointed myself as a silent protector, lying awake at night listening for any burglar that might be out and about.

In the new house mice had taken over. So, we spent some time listening to the sound of snapping traps at night, knowing we were closing in on a mouse free house. The house hadn't been occupied for a while before we bought it. Dad had gotten a good deal on the house he'd said. No one knew why at the time, but we found out later and it was unusual.

I entered Mrs. Lizwetczky's second grade class for the last month and a half of the school year. If nothing else her name challenged me to improve spelling skills. Robinson Grade School was set high at one end, bordered by a red brick wall, the same colored brick used for the building itself, topped off with a black iron grate. The grate wasn't there to keep kids in or out, but from falling onto the sidewalk below. The rest of the schoolyard was open to sidewalk areas. Behind the school we played softball on an asphalt playground in gym class and marbles around front in the dirt yard. The school has surrendered the front yard to asphalt where many rounds of marbles had been played.

Marbles aren't popular, anymore. The school is still standing east of Hoban High School, looking down I-76 at the Fourth Street exit near Goodyear's Plant I and its Reclaim Plant.

I had friends from Robinson and in our neighborhood on Talbot. A boy across the street, named Billy Beaver was a year or two older. We liked the same things, in general, and found less trouble to get into than the friends my brother had found. Brother distanced himself from me, growing faster and a lot taller at the time – he thought of me as his little brother. In fact, the neighborhood called me "Little Henry," and my brother Bobby, "Big Henry." From the time we lived at Grandma's his friends were my friends, but not any longer.

When school was out we readjusted to the city ways, once again, but always kept our slingshot at the ready. We were threatened not once, but many times with seizure of the home-made weapon. But trees were plentiful as were rubber inner tubes then, so we didn't suffer outages for long. We kept them out of sight stashed with our bean shooters.

The bean shooter caused me to get into it with Mom about my get-even attitude and lack of skill at concealment. On the driveway side adjacent to our house lived three old maids, said to be sisters. They were old for sure, always complaining we were in their yard or about something we had done. I can't remember what. Seeking to even things up one evening at dusk I decided to pester the old maids by shooting beans at their kitchen window that faced our kitchen window. From my station at the corner of our back porch, I fired salvos at the transparent target. Thinking they'd have no idea what was causing the repeated snapping at their window, I shot the beans in bursts then ducked out of sight next to our porch. I thought it was foolproof – it wasn't. The sisters must have teamed up taking counter offensive positions at different windows of the second floor and attic floor landing to solve the mysterious snapping sound. I thought it would be seen by them as a phenomenon. I caught a glimpse of a curtain moving in the second floor window during my last salvo. I quickly ducked around the corner. I waited. Nothing happened. I fired again. Then I heard a phone ring.

The screen door swung open. I was in the process of sighting in the window to launch more missiles. Well, you know what happened next. Mom grabbed me by the ear and in the old maid's kitchen all three of them stood over me, bearing down like buzzards about to land on their prey. After turning over my "shooter" ammunition – a full bag of beans – and apologizing, I wasn't any more popular with them than before. I think we had a meeting of the minds that night. They didn't complain as much, although their curtains ruffled when I walked between the houses, and I didn't have to apologize to them anymore. When Dad got home I was surprised to learn he had just gotten a new belt.

It seemed relatives were showing up with regularity on Talbot, more than they ever had before. They seemed in awe of the mansion. The Eddleman's, my mom's twin sister, Esther, and her family; the Granger's, my mom's older sister's family; the Erwin's, my mom's brother's family, Uncle Kenny, the motorcycle rider and my favorite uncle; the Markovich's, my dad's sister, Maxine's family; the Willard Henry's, my dad's oldest brother who'd seen jail from the inside; George Henry, who'd just gotten out of prison due to robbing a gas station, some said; Bob, the entertainer; and Lyle, my dad's youngest brother; of course Grandma Erwin, who was always welcome wherever we were; and Dad's parents, Grandma and Grandpa Henry. Grandpa was usually with Grandma when he was sober – we didn't see him very often. I think we had a better house than they all did at the time, but things would change for the Henrys as a new law reared its head and sent things awry for quite a while. Dad began using a term that surfaced from time-to-time when misfortune came along; the term – Henry's Law. I found out later there really is a "Henry's Law." The law of physics named after an English chemist, William Henry. The law isn't about misfortune or luck, but rather about the nature of solubility of gases in liquids.

It was during this time at the end of the second grade at Robinson in late spring of 1948, that I lost my color-blindness. Its significance involved colored people. The school population was nearly twenty percent "colored," as African Americans were called then, and had called themselves. It was better than the other name used derisively at that time. I soon learned most people looked down on them as a class of people. As far as the percent of students economically depressed were concerned, I think all of us at Robinson were to some extent disadvantaged. But, the degree of economic disadvantage was more apparent and I learned we had come up in the world from where we were, and from those around us. Color was an important factor and colored people were far less advantaged then, than they are now, since heavy emphasis has been placed on equality.

My first real encounter with this difference came at the end of second grade. I had just put my pen back in the ink well where I had dropped a couple of white navy beans – shooter beans. The beans produced a healthy green bean sprout growing out of the opening. I took notice of a dangling pigtail near my inkwell from the girl's hair sitting in front of me.

The girl was a colored girl who I talked with every day. I gently tugged on the pigtail. She turned around and gave me a menacing look. I was being playful and thought, "She isn't having any fun," so I did it again. She went to the pencil sharpener, returned to her desk; this time when she turned around she grabbed my hand and jabbed a number two pencil into the palm of my hand. The lead broke off and lodged into my palm. It drew blood. I jumped from the pain, startled and shocked by her attack. It seemed highly inappropriate to the level of pain, if any, I had inflicted on her. I leaned over and said, "You're a 'coon'." I was mad as hell, and so was she. The commotion drew the teacher's attention. Soon I was seated in the Principal's office. He, too, was colored. My mother was called in and I got a lesson from both, as I dug the lead out of my hand, still mad. I thought the girl was my friend. I was perplexed by the action she took.

Mom had always preached no one is any better than anyone else. I thought that's not really the way things were, but I agreed then and now, this is basically true. No circumstance should deny anyone the right to achieve and to become whatever he or she wants to be. And secondly, don't judge anyone by what they are at present, but by what they are trying to do. Because it seems to me – it's not what one is by birth that counts, but what one is ever striving to become.

Color of my parents also became of interest. Dad had a darker complexion with coal-black hair. Mom was a blue-eyed blonde with a fair complexion. No one believed my brother and I were, in fact, brothers. It occurred so often it had caused me some concern. We were opposites in coloration like our parents, and in other ways. Brother always got into fights, while I tried to avoid them. I began to wonder if I was a sissy. Dad was tough and had gotten into a fight in the driveway at Grandma's when we lived there. I wanted dark eyes, dark hair, and wanted to be a tough guy, too.

The two sides of the family followed the same pattern. It gave me some comfort. Uncle Kenny was a tough guy. He had light blonde red hair with a ruddy complexion. Therefore, I thought you didn't need dark hair to be tough after all. He rode big Indians and Harleys and scared the hell out of everybody with his drinking, fighting, and studded black leather jacket. Dad liked Uncle Kenny. I found out later they had chummed around together before my mom and dad got married. Still, my fair complexion and light blonde hair bothered me for some time, but I eventually got over it.

I had no concept of what it was like to be a Negro, colored from birth, a minority. I empathized with my colored friends, Beasley, Clark, Cherry, and Bently in Niles, Ohio, where Grandma was living now. Each I had to fight at different times; Clark over the pigtail incident, the others for reasons hard to remember now, only that it happened. I grew to like colored people depending on what they were trying to become, like many of us. It wasn't easy for them or us.

The summer of '48 we were in danger of losing the house on Talbot. I was a busy little guy, building soapbox derby's that never got their wheels, save for unwanted tricycle wheels salvaged from the dump at the bottom of Whitney Street. I didn't take enough time for personal needs often enough and found it boring sitting on the toilet longer than normal, suffering constipation to make up for the infrequency. To occupy my time I'd use a knife to whittle on wood. On this sunny day, I sat there lighting paper matches and throwing them between my legs listening to them hiss as they drowned. I always had a pack of matches in my pocket. I was highly experienced with applying flame to newspaper and brown grocery bags; bags burned slowly enough to throw off hot sparks in the night sky. If you wadded and twisted the bags together in a spiral and waved the bags skyward, the sparks would travel upward until they expired.

To the left white toilet tissue hung below a half-open window decorated with a pair of pink colored cloth curtains that overlaid a beige-colored blind. The blind would snap up when you pulled it down and let go quickly. Having done that a few times, I lit a match to see how toilet paper burns. No sooner had the flame touched the end of the tissue than the bright orange opiate leaped up the paper roll and caught the curtains on fire. I mimicked the flames and leaped up, batting the curtains with one hand and pulling up my pants with the other. The fire was winning the battle. Smoke rolled out the half-open window and curled around the ceiling. This didn't look good.

Mom was outside talking with the old maids. They saw the smoke pouring out of the window and darkening the side of the house. When she rushed into the bathroom I was swinging a towel at the growing inferno. She grabbed another towel, threw it in the bathtub and turned the water on. We both battled the flames and smoke, my pants gathered around my ankles, my mom frantic amid all the shrieking. In a bit, after the highly flammables had been consumed, the fire slowed enough for us to dowse the painted trim window molding and built-in drawers at the corner across from the toilet. She glared at me when the coughing, screaming, and frenzy subsided. Half of the bathroom and ceiling was blackened, the blind and curtains were ashes, woodwork scorched, smoke blackened my face and my hair was singed. By the way, toilet tissue burns real good.

At that point shrill sirens signaled the maid's interference again. They must have called the fire department. The fire was out at 429 Talbot, but here they were, three firemen standing in our bathroom shaking their heads. I kind of remember thinking I took after my dad's brother, Uncle Bob, the entertainer.

Mom took on a new role, the enforcer, since Dad wouldn't be home for a day or two from a trip. It started a new trend my brother didn't like much. She gave it to me with Dad's old belt. When he got home, he gave it to me with his new belt. Things were better when he worked at Red Star; he came home every night and we only got it once. But, in all fairness I almost burned the house down. The politics only seemed unfair; double jeopardy wouldn't be a suitable defense in our house.

In the fall I entered third grade, Mrs. Tidyman's class, a little worse for the summer wear. One of my friends, Don Stewart, invited me to a Halloween party at his church. Mom let me go thinking church wouldn't hurt and might help me mend my wayward ways. She tore up some old clothes and when she finished a pirate stared back at me in the mirror. In her mind it fit my scalawag nature. The party wasn't significant in itself and I don't remember much about it, but the church would influence me for some time to come. The church, The Salvation Army, was located in a run-down, red asphalt shingled, two-story building at 1104 Johnston Street in East Akron, about seven blocks from Talbot Avenue.

Mom encouraged me to join the Cub Scouts when I came home one day from school and told her some friends were joining a neighborhood pack. She thought like church, it might improve my citizenship. I guess it did. They taught us a lot of things like tying knots and some I took to naturally, like – how to start fires.

At Christmas time the school permitted gift exchanges among the classmates. I thought it was a great opportunity to receive something good – a surprise. I shopped with my mom to pick out a gift for the name I'd drawn. There was a limit, of course. Gifts may have consisted of nothing more than a coloring book with crayons, or a water color paint set, but it was a surprise. I drew a girl's name and Buster got mine. On the day of the exchange, I anxiously awaited my gift. Upon tearing open the wrapping paper I found a black plastic hand-held Viewmaster. You held it to the light and looked through a magnifying porthole for sighting at little pictures called celluloid slides. I was puzzled. It was scratched, one corner was broken off and the lever to change pictures was jammed. There were no slides included. Was this a present? Was this intentional?

At home I showed my disappointment. I was beginning to dislike surprises.

"Who is Buster?" Mom asked.

"A kid from Children's Home."

"Oh," she said, nodding her head. "Donny, they don't have parents and he probably didn't have any money to spend for a gift. He couldn't buy you anything."

"Other kids from the Home gave kids some good stuff. There are three of 'em in our class," I said.

"Just be happy we were able to get a nice gift for your exchange present. Be glad you have parents and don't feel like that. Feel bad for Buster and be sure you thank him."

Buster was a bully, but I did as Mom told me to do. When I got to school the next day I felt bad for him after all. I thanked him, genuinely, for the present.

Buster laughed.

I still had another chance. The Cub Scout Pack also scheduled a gift exchange with other Packs at a big Christmas get-together. So my mom and I were off again to pick out another gift for some lucky kid. We went to the 5 and 10 cent store on Arlington Street where I convinced her to buy a plastic dart gun with four darts and a target. It was something any boy my age would want. We got home and she wrapped it in brightly colored red paper.

When the Cub Packs were ready for the exchange, it was decided all gifts would go to the center table in the auditorium, placed there by each cub. Dutifully, I marched up and carefully placed the bright red package on the table. I kept my eyes on the package after returning to my seat. No one took it. A number of cubs picked it up but laid it back down. I didn't think I'd ever get a chance to pick out a surprise, there were so many kids in the auditorium. I twisted and turned in my seat waiting for our pack's turn to go to the table. When it finally came around to our pack's turn, no one had taken mine, yet, from among the hundred, or so, brightly colored packages. Quickly calculating the odds of finding something better than a dart gun set, and with the recent Buster experience as a guide, I directed my feet to Mom's neatly wrapped surprise. I grabbed my own gift, before anyone else had a chance and swiftly returned to my seat.

Mom looked at the package, puzzled. "That's ours, isn't it?"

"I don't know. Is it?" I asked innocently.

"Let me see that," she said.

I flashed the package, but held on.

Before she could say, "Take it back," I'd ripped open the paper to guarantee a good prize this time. I got what I wanted and was certain there wasn't anything better on the table. My brother and I had great fun shouting, "Bulls eyes," licking the rubber suction cups at the end of the darts and shooting each other close-up on the forehead, where they stuck real good. It was the first time I'd rigged a gift exchange. First time for rigging anything. It was a fair exchange; no one took the gift, so, I did. I was learning.

The third grade stands out as a year in which the teacher, Mrs. Tidyman, recognized my art ability. If I wasn't talking, I was drawing. I rushed through most schoolwork so I could get to the never ending supply of paper, paint and colored chalk. It was also the year I received my first and only de-lousing. Notices sent home warned of an outbreak of head lice. Everyone was asked to get a prescription to cure it. The stuff stunk and burned my head as Mom poured the solution on my scalp over the sink. I was certain it would leave me hairless and brainless while the medicine fried the little pests. To top it off, no one said my brother or I had lice. We both got the treatment anyway. It was preventative medicine at its best. There was something low-class about lice I became aware of, somehow.

I celebrated the close of the school on June 9, 1949, my ninth birthday, by passing out and slipping from my desk to the varnished wooden floor. As I was sprawled on the floor I remember opening my eyes and staring between the cast iron desk legs at people legs and shoes. Mrs. Tidyman and other teachers were standing over me to see what was happening to this third grader who had passed out. Some birthday.

"Donny, can you get up?" Mrs. Tidyman asked.

I could hear, but couldn't answer. I was groggy.

"Do you want to get up?" she urged.

"No," I finally responded.

Even with a choice, I couldn't move. I fell unconscious again.

The next thing I remember was lying in the back seat of a car. Andy the gym teacher drove me home. The school must have called Mom because she rushed out crying as Andy carried me up the steps and into the house. He laid me on the couch.

"The nurse checked him out," Andy said. "He seems okay now, but we think you should take him to a doctor. The nurse said he must have had a convulsion."

"Did the nurse say anything else?" Mom asked, trembling and worried.

"She doesn't know anything more. He was on the floor a while – see what the doctor says.

He's probably okay." Andy looked at me, "Aren't you, tough guy?"

I liked Andy, especially for saying "Tough guy."

Mom got on the phone and talked to neighbors to see if someone had a car available to take us to a doctor nearby. After a couple of calls a neighbor across the street was more than willing to help. She dropped us off in front of Dr. Beatty's office, on the second floor above a Rexall drug store on the corner of Fourth Street and Arlington. The doctor gave me a once-over exam, thumped on my chest and listened to sounds through a stethoscope. When he was done he sat back in his squeaky chair, looked at Mom and said, "He'll live." That was quite good to hear. Mom was relieved. As far as a diagnosis he thought I had a nervous exhaustion attack, prompted by the excitement of the last day of school and my birthday all at once. True, I was excited about getting out of school, but the birthday didn't mean that much.   Perhaps I should have told him about the things that were going "bump in the night" at home, keeping me awake all night.

We all heard the sounds. They came from the second floor bedroom hallway area and the stairs to the attic. It took a while for each family member to make the others aware of the strange and eerie sounds. Eventually, something was revealed that surprised us all.

I built stick-model airplanes in our attic. Cardboard boxes were set up as a table for the plans placed under a swinging bare light bulb suspended from the ceiling. Late into the night I'd work turning out WWII fighter planes. More than once, as I sat with my back to the two flights of stairs, I heard footsteps. I was surprised to find no one there. Imagination I thought. Squeaking wood, I thought. Sleepy, I thought. Lying awake in my second floor bedroom with my brother asleep on other nights the sound of footsteps, floor squeaks at regular intervals, then up the attic stairs, more squeaks – I'd hold my breath and listen.

I told Brother. He said he heard the noises. We chalked it up as normal things for an old house. Nothing for two tough kids to be worried about.

429 Talbot Ave After 1952

Later we learned Dad had heard curious things in the hallway off of our bedrooms. He called out, "Bobby?" Donny?" No one responded. He got out of bed, then checked our rooms. He thought one of us might be sleepwalking and decided to look after hearing the bathroom door open and footsteps cease at that point. When he checked we were in bed, sleeping. The noises continued. I had several nightmares causing me to scream, waking up everyone. But, it was only "The Mummy" and "Frankenstein" that had visited my dreams, nothing as real as the ghostly noises in our house.

We didn't find out about Dad's story for several years after we'd moved from the house. Upon returning to visit neighbors we were told the people who bought our house had moved out because of ghosts. A neighbor who we didn't talk with much when we lived there revealed a murder had occurred in the house. An older couple lived there as the story goes – the man killed the woman. The reason for the good deal Dad had gotten when he bought the house was made clear. A few years later during a drive-by visit to the old neighborhood I found the house no longer there. The old maid's house was still there, as were the others, but our house was gone. The basement had been filled-in and the trees in the backyard were still standing, but the spot our house had occupied was now a vacant weed-filled lot.

I learned more about life's problems during the summer between third and fourth grades. It was a time when bums still appeared in neighborhoods, from nowhere, relatives appeared from everywhere, and I went to work as a shoeshine boy in front of a local bar at the corner of Arlington and Fifth Avenue, the Penguin Bar.

The bum looked like a bum should look as far as I knew. He came from the alley behind the house. I was taking apart an orange crate, board-by-board, straightening the nails to be reused for anything that came to mind. He wore a brown hat, a rumpled brown oversized suit – why do bums always wear suits – and carried a small suitcase with him. The suit draped over his skinny frame, too hot for summer and showcased a dangling colorful long tie, flopping on his yellowing white shirt. He smiled at me.

I squinted in the sun, looked up and smiled back at him. I noticed he needed a shave but otherwise he looked cleaned up.

"Is mommy home?" he asked.

"Um-hmm," I responded, wondering if I should say, no.

I began to feel threatened and felt a need to protect Mom. I stopped unbending nails on the brick and gripped the hammer tightly. I watched him walk up to the back porch and rap on the screen door.

Mom appeared. She said, "Yes?"

He removed his hat displaying his gray hair. "Ma'am. I've been down on my luck and need some work. Anything I can do to earn some food? Anything will do."

Mom studied him for a second or two. "Sure, I can get you something."

"No, Ma'am. I don't want a hand-out. I'll work for it, if you tell me what you need done. I'm good at a lot of things," he said.

"Wait a minute," she said.

The bum stood there, with hat in hand, staring into the house. Mom returned and said, "The front porch needs swept. And, you can do the back porch, too." She opened the screen door and handed him a broom.

"Thank you, Ma'am." He went around front between the old maid's and our house.

I put the hammer down and went into the kitchen. Mom had gotten bread and began making a sandwich. I sat down, watching. "Why does he have to ask for something, Mom?"

"He doesn't have a job, Donny."

"Why not?"

"I don't know," she said.

"The porch didn't need swept."

"I know."

"Why'd you tell him to do it, then?"

"Donny, he just wants something to eat. That's the least we can do," she said.

She finished the preparation. Shortly, the bum came up on the back porch. He swished the broom across the small porch. When he finished, I wondered if Mom was going to let him inside. She didn't. She had enough street sense to keep him outside, I thought.

She handed him a plate with two sandwiches and a glass of milk. He thanked her and took a seat on the top step. I watched him through the screen door. He didn't take his hat off and quickly downed the food. He stretched. He got up and approached the screen door.

"Could I see your mommy, again, please?"

"Mom," I yelled.

"Are you through?" Mom asked.

"Yes, Ma'am. It was very good."

She opened the screen door and took the empty plate and glass.

"Thank you, and bless you," he said.

Mom handed him a dollar and some change.

"Bless you and thank you. You're very kind," he said. The bum tipped his hat. His suit ruffled as he went down the steps.

I watched Mom hook the screen door. "Where's he going?" I asked.

"I don't know," Mom said, watching him step into the alley and disappear among the trees on his way south.

"We have to help people like that." She stared at the alley a while then went upstairs to finish her work.

The old man who had come to our backyard was a gentleman, polite in every way and didn't deserve to be a bum. It made me stop and think about what happens to good people like that.

Mom's dad, Grandpa Erwin, had visited us the year before for a day or two on leave from the "home." He sat on the back porch in a rocker and smoked a corncob pipe. Only months earlier before the bum appeared in our backyard, she received word he died. I believe she was thinking of her father when she prepared the sandwiches for the man in the brown suit, who was "down on his luck." The bum looked to be the same age as her father at the time. A few years from then, I was wondering what I'd be doing for money. But for now, I was satisfied with engaging my skills as a shoeshine boy. I selected a spot at the Penguin Bar, on the corner of Arlington and Fifth Avenue.

The corner had high foot traffic. A bus stop on a corner was dominated by a gas station where I filled my bicycle tires with air, a church across from it, the United Brethren, and the Arlington Lumber Company across the street from the Penguin Bar. I'd set-up just outside the door of the bar on the sidewalk. "Hey, you want a shine?" I'd call out to the drunks as they came out. They seemed to be in a much better state of mind than most passersby, and more agreeable to a shine. At first my work was all done on the sidewalk, including male and female clients. It must have been apparent my skills were not innate. No formal training had shown in my snapping and buffing technique,

Grandpa Erwin on back porch

because the finished product wasn't much better than the shine of the shoe originally presented on my shoeshine box built from an orange crate.

Nevertheless, some of the Penguin's regular customers became my regulars and they invited me inside to ply my trade. They'd hike up on a shiny red plastic covered bar stool, drop a foot on my box and smile a lot. There were a lot of smiles. I was cheap live entertainment, a generally agreeable sort of companion. The smell of the beer, laughter, and liveliness attracted me, but it was the kind of place Mom wouldn't have approved, at all. When she found out I was going into the bar and receiving some good tips, charging a dime, but getting twenty-five to fifty cents, she put an end to my employment and forbade me to pursue my new-found career.

Brother and I had to move to the attic when Aunt Esther and her family moved in with us. The arrangement was necessary to help them out. Uncle Melvin had a knack for not being able to find jobs. It was on-going. Mom always helped her twin in one way or another for as long as I can remember. Aunt Esther was a lot like Mom. I liked her.

The Eddleman's didn't stay with us for long and the attic bedroom was soon vacated in favor of our own bedrooms back down on the second floor.

I came to understand men should work. There were too many examples of what happens to families when men don't work. Some people try to get around working, preferring drinking and welfare to holding a steady job.

My dad always worked, and broke the trend in our family.

1949 to 1952

"Tuffy Duffy" became my fourth grade teacher and had a reputation for being mean. I wasn't looking forward to this school year, after such a pleasant teacher from the year before. Looking back, I think I had a crush on Mrs. Tidyman. She always had a bright smile when you talked with her and she calmed down the unruly class. I don't know anyone who had gotten the "Board of Education" paddling in her class. Most teachers mounted the symbol of misbehaving high on the wall in front of the class, but not high up enough it couldn't be reached quickly.

Mrs. Duffy would be different. She was much older, cotton-like white hair, powdered and rouged face, like a Kabuki and most of all, stern. Tuffy taught us discipline. I sat up straight and listened to everything she had to say. The attention resulted from watching Mrs. Duffy whack kids with a paddle in front of the class – she kept the paddle at the side of her desk – and Buster getting his mouth washed out with soap for swearing. I earned the best grades in her class. I also led the class in her bonus grading system. The system consisted of a special weekly test that centered on current events and questions not covered in any of the class work. It became necessary to read the newspaper every night and clip articles. You advanced as far as possible without missing a question. If you missed a question, it was up to you to find the answer and to try again the next week. I led the class, two or three questions ahead of everyone else, even those who were considered brains. I gained a reputation for being smart. I liked the label, but didn't let on. In reality fear spurred my education and drove me to the head of the class. Even so, I didn't become the teacher's pet because I also felt the sting of her paddle on occasion.

One day Mrs. Duffy stood in front of the class, three desks in front of mine and to the left, and said something astounding at the time. "Someday, someone in this class may become President of the United States." She hoped that one of her students might do just that – what a challenge. I believe she took her role seriously hoping to have a small part in shaping a future President. To her it must not have been impossible. As I looked around the room at my colored friends, and Buster, thought of my own background, it didn't seem likely. We didn't dare laugh, although a couple of eye exchanges danced a little at the far away thought. Knowing the status of her "charges," she focused mostly on Abraham Lincoln's underprivileged life and his necessity to read by the light of a log cabin fireplace as a good example for us.

I never thought much about it after that, thinking Mrs. Duffy was a little old and she didn't really believe it could happen. As I got older and found out what is required to become the President, it became apparent that, in the first place, she was right, there was a possibility. In the second place, it wasn't probable – and so far, I was right.

It seemed I was always talking as had been disclosed on my report card in the second grade at Roosevelt Grade School.

I was always asking questions getting me into trouble with my mom, dad, and my brother's friends. In the spring after a history of chronic sore throats, there came a time for reflection in a hospital bed after a tonsillectomy. I couldn't talk. The date was May 10, 1950. I thought I was going to die. I reviewed in my mind why people seemed to be annoyed with me. My never ending questions and incessant talking was the basis for the minor problem. My dad, more than once, said, "You're always asking questions. I can't think." The criticism usually came when he was working on his truck, building things, or doing things that puzzled me. I can remember asking him why the sky was blue, and he kind of chuckled, with sweat on his brow looked up and said – "I don't know," with a smile. They were important things – it's the ozone in the air I found out. Since he was well-liked I observed everything he did. He had the black hair and didn't talk much as contrasted with Mom and me. With the new found discipline administered in Mrs. Duffy's fourth grade who admonished us to "listen and learn," I decided to embark on a philosophy that would reduce my vocalizations to bare minimums. This new behavior was established and fixed while lying in a hospital bed at St. Thomas Hospital, where Dr. Zeno, a brother of the owners of Dad's company, separated my tonsils and adenoids from me forever.

Limited discourse seemed the only approach to take after analyzing the problem carefully. Gary Cooper didn't say much in the movies, and used "yup" and "nope" to great advantage. I had been mulling over the problem for some time now, had studied other leading men, mostly cowboys – but throw in Alan Ladd and Cary Grant at the Cameo Theater on Arlington Street – taking note of how much they talked and how many questions they asked. It seemed better to wait for others to talk, if asked a question to say as little as possible. At that time I became determined to be a yup and nope man upon leaving the hospital. To this day, I basically have been a non-verbal person, preferring to listen and let others do the talking, waiting for the right opportunity to jump in and add detail to present unknown facts, or as a back-up to anyone's deficiencies with additional information. If I'm uninformed, I shut up and listen. However, there are times when I forget my pledge and revert to my second grade self, but then something makes me stop and I slip back into the hospital bed of my mind and clam up. After coming home from the hospital I was able to talk, but didn't. My mom was the only one who caught on to the drastic change. The others must have been grateful. They didn't want to say anything to get me going.

"How come you're not taking much?" she asked. "Does your throat hurt?"

"Nope," I said.

"Why aren't you saying much, then?"

"Nothin' to say."

"Why?" she asked.

"Cause," I replied after studying her question.

Finally, after a couple days of the third degree on the couch I told her about my plan to listen more and talk less. She laughed, tried to talk me out of it, but saw I was serious. She realized I was on the verge of growing up and she wouldn't do anything to stop me. A while ago, it had been said about a couple of relatives that they didn't know when to stop talking. They wouldn't let anyone get a word in "edgewise." I assumed my talking too much was one of those family afflictions, but I wanted cured.

When school was out my brother heard about an older couple, the Taylor's on Third Street, who hired kids to sell home-made doughnuts. It appeared to me this would be a real opportunity to acquire cash for my stick models. The routes were nearby, I didn't need a bicycle and it was a good way to spend the summer. I had just turned ten, too young for the job. They said the cut-off point was twelve years, which we knew but I had to find a way around it. It didn't bother me, being twelve and saying I was twelve. It was two entirely different things. The Taylor's had graying hair and were thin soft-spoken people and reminded me of very nice grandparents. They advertised their product on white printed bags and on a sign that was attached over their front porch, "Taylor's Home Made Doughnuts." They hadn't made up the slogan as I had my age. They must have needed kids and took me in. The doughnuts were, literally, made in several rooms on the first floor of their home; the kitchen, dining room, and living room where deep-fat frying equipment and various ovens were installed.

I arrived early for my inventory, usually two peck baskets filled with an assortment of glazed, chocolate iced, plain, powdered, and cinnamon packed in one-half, one dozen, and two dozen white bags. They cooked them each morning. As I waited for my supply, I watched the intriguing process. The dough machine plopped circles into the hot deep-fat fryer. Immediately the circles puffed up, were moved along by a wire mesh divider then automatically flipped over to fry on the opposite side. After cooking they were scooped out of the hot oil and cooled, before the icings and flavorings were applied.

We went out on our routes two mornings a week and on Saturday, the day for big sales. Our pay was ten cents a dozen sold, which was generous considering the price for a dozen doughnuts brought thirty-five cents. Occasionally, we'd get a nickel or dime tip which was the cost of a small stick-model airplane kit or admission to the Cameo for as long as you wanted to stay. We'd start out at nine a.m. It would take us until noon or later to cover our route. It was fun and yet hard work, lugging the filled baskets, one in each hand, up and down the sidewalks and onto the porches of each home. My sales pitch hadn't changed much from my shoeshine days, "Wanna buy some doughnuts?" A natural sales pitch seemed to suffice – there were only a few times my baskets contained unsold inventory.

I became familiar with the territory. As the newness of the job wore off, I would get hungry before finishing the route. One Saturday morning at the end of the route, I had one half-dozen, and two of the largest bags left. Hunger got the best of me. I figured both two-dozen bags wouldn't sell and if I took a doughnut, I'd pay the Taylors' for the doughnut. So, I sat down on a sculptured cement block retaining wall in front of a house I'd just solicited. I munched away on a powdered doughnut. Without anything to drink I was thirsty in the hot noon-day sun and the doughnut hard to swallow, but it did the trick. I plodded up the walk to the next house. The lady bought one of the two dozen bags. There were only a couple of homes to go – I didn't think it likely any more would be sold. To my surprise, the lady in the last house of the day wanted three dozen. Wow, three dozen, but all I had was the half-dozen bag and the two dozen bag, less one. She wanted them all. I scratched my head, wondering if I should tell her about the missing doughnut, but decided it might ruin the sale somehow. She could have all of the doughnuts less one!

The lady handed me the money and I turned around walking fast, then faster, but not quite fast enough. I didn't get any more than four sidewalk squares away from her front walk when she opened the door yelling, "Hey, kid, stop!" I didn't look back. She kept yelling as I scrambled to get out of there. Well, I ran. I couldn't believe she had opened the bags and counted every doughnut, every last one. The odds of that happening at the instant she went inside must be staggering. The odds of me getting hungry at that time and selling nearly three dozen doughnuts, equally staggering. Henry's Law, maybe. At any rate, the odds were too great for me to hang around and find out why. After all, it only amounted to three cents. She could see my baskets were empty. What was the big deal, anyway? I was muttering to myself as my conscience got the best of me going back to Taylor's.

When I turned the baskets and money over to Mr. Taylor, I told him somebody might call about a missing powdered doughnut. He simply deducted the three cents from my pay. I expected a scolding from Mr. Taylor, but he only asked, "Did you like the doughnut?" The lady must have decided not to press charges, they didn't hear from her as far as I know. Over the next week I skipped by her house, letting her cool off. The next time I stopped at her house she asked me if she could have an extra doughnut to make up for the missing one. Things ended up okay.

My dad got restless with his employment at Zeno Brothers. He began investigating the possibility of going into business for himself. He wanted to buy a tractor and flatbed trailer to haul steel as an independent broker between steel mills, warehouses, and customers wherever a "load" could be found. He knew other drivers who'd done this a year or two earlier and were doing well. Burgy was one of his friends doing the same thing. It became the subject of discussions between Mom and Dad for a while. As with any new idea, once you "get the bug" to strike out on your own, the reasons for not doing it are never as exciting, or as convincing, as those in favor of doing it. "You have to try, don't you?"

As this new prospect germinated, Dad's bother, Willard, needed assistance for some reason. So, my brother and I returned to school and retreated back to the attic to make room for Uncle Willard's family. My dad retreated into his imagination as he was about to take the biggest step in his life and lay plans for going into business for himself.

During the fifth grade, somewhere around the middle of the year, January 1951, Uncle Willard's family moved out. A brand new, bright red REO tractor showed up in the driveway of our house. Normally it would be parked in the back of our house where Dad, earlier, had cut a driveway through from the alley to park Zeno's truck. Dad had gone from Red Star, to

Zeno's and now had become an independent steel hauler. Each time he changed jobs our standard of living had risen. Mobility appeared to be a good thing. In his new job, he was gone for a week or more at times, depending on snow and availability of loads. It took a toll on Mom.

About this time I took an interest in girls. In Mrs. Brass's fifth grade class a girl caught my eye. She had curly coal-black hair, and for the first time, a girl who wore lipstick in class. With her raven hair, dark complexion, and red lipstick, I had a hard time keeping my mind on the three R's or whatever was being taught at the time. Of course I told no one, keeping it all out of sight. I was shy around girls. My conversation wasn't sparkling given an occasional "yup" or "nope." She was a brain and never knew of my attraction, but I found ways to stray into her neighborhood on Fourth Street near Robinson school hoping to catch sight of her outside – signs of a young stalker. Later, I ran into her at Kent State where I had transferred from the University of Akron for a short time. She had changed – her hair clipped short and a little straighter than I remembered, her lips natural now, petite, but still pretty. Funny how things change, but memories don't.

The year moved along. We survived the big snow of '51, about three feet high in drifts, but the situation worsened for Dad. He had difficulty when steel began to slow down. Having relatives live with us in the mansion was an adjustment, but now the prospect of boarders became an opportunity to help with finances. It started with a lumber truck delivering some two-by-eights and four-by-fours to our back yard. Dad got his hand saw – he never had any power tools – and began building. I always liked working with him, building things. I sat there throughout the effort, handing him this and that as the structure progressed. He must have noticed I wasn't asking questions like I used to do, because at different intervals he'd ask me questions.

"Know what I'm doing, now?"

"Nope."

"I'm building stairs."

No comment, no questions.

"Know why?" he asked.

"Nope."

"We're going to rent out the upstairs."

I simply nodded.

That's the way it got started. The early validation of Henry's Law swung into action. Dad went into debt to purchase the red REO and flatbed trailer to seek his fortune right at the time the economy slowed, just before a prolonged steel strike, idling thousands of workers and affecting thousands of others associated with it, including the Henry family.

"Laws are made to be broken," a not-so-wise man once speculated as he was being hauled into jail. Henry's Law on the other hand worked in mundane ways, as experienced by victims who had given it an aura of authenticity – something to count on when things were going sideways. Like a lonely trucker on a two lane winding road and moonless night at three o'clock in the morning bearing down on a narrow older bridge. In the distance over a hill headlights approach. Then the trucker enters one end of the bridge, the other vehicle enters the other end and they meet, simultaneously, head-on at the center of the bridge. The chance encounter causes stressful seconds as they slip by each other in the silence of the night. No one scrapes or bumps the other, blood pressures ease. The road jiggles on in front of the trucker's headlights. The unplanned event was like the two dozen and a half doughnuts, less one. Staggering odds.

Neither the truck nor the bridge operates under any Law. It's the luck of the draw, the chance of the circumstance. The genesis of all events are either coincidence or planning, sometimes both. "The harder I work, the luckier I get," some say. Destiny is only offered as a supposition in the absence of knowledge, forecasted intuition based on random facts in a pattern to fit the supposition. Henry's Law is only bad luck that is reinforced over time. Everyone gets their share while some never seem to collect any.

I was ten years old and already had experienced a couple of near misses. Misses that could have stopped the clock for me, before a near drowning incident happened in Niles in 1951. The events I'm describing now occurred in 1950.

Dad had taken Bobby with him to let him see what he did for a living as the owner of a brokerage company hauling steel with his new trailer and tractor, the red REO. The trip began in the evening around six-thirty and lasted until the sun came up the next morning. If my brother got sleepy, he would have to sleep on the bench seat beside Dad, while he drove to drop-offs in different cities. When the big rig truck driver and the kid came home from the night's work, Bobby was excited. He had a great time. He told Mom and me all about the trip with Dad.

Of course I was promised that I would get to go on a trip with my dad a little later. I couldn't wait to do the same thing Bobby had done.

My trip day had arrived. I climbed up onto the footboard of the shiny red REO, turned the handle of the door and entered the cabin of the truck. The smell of new rubber mats and the vinyl bench seat was strong, but provided an agreeable aroma to my way of thinking. The smell was similar to the smell of burned coffee on most nights emanating from Goodyear's reclaim factory near Robinson Grade School. I jumped on the seat and closed the heavy door. I felt grown up. The trip started out about the same time in the evening as Bobby's did. Dad backed the tractor out of the drive where he parked the REO behind our house, turned the big steering wheel, put it in gear and we traveled south for a short distance down the alley, turned right onto Arlington Street on our way to hook up with the flatbed trailer he stored in a lot about ten blocks down Arlington. At the lot we got out. Dad told me to watch the fifth wheel when he backed the tractor up to lock his tractor and trailer together.

That was neat – I gave Dad a thumbs up. I got back into the truck and we headed east toward Youngstown, Ohio, where Steel mills were located. On the way we traveled through the country on State Route 18, the way we drove to Niles many times. Before we got very far I spied a white stork standing on alert, looking for dinner in a swampy pond area. "Look, there's a stork," I said. Dad said, "It's an egret." This trip was getting off to an interesting good start. I had never seen a live white egret before. I always called them storks.

After an hour's driving, we pulled into a large open doorway inside a steel warehouse on the outskirts but close to the steel mills in Youngstown. Dad said we were getting a load of square steel tubing in bundles. A crane was going to pick up the steel bundles and place them on the trailer. He told me to stay in the truck and not get out, it wouldn't take long. Dad went into an office door to get paperwork. I turned around to watch the overhead crane come and go with bundles, stacking them up on the flatbed. I had never seen raw steel that large before. I heard different loud noises inside the warehouse and clanking from the bundles being stacked. At one point the cab shook. Dad ran out of the office and quickly tore open the door.

"Get out," he shouted with terror enveloping his eyes.

He yanked me out of the truck like a bundle of hay and pulled me along with him.

"What's wrong? Dad, what's wrong?"

"I shouldn't have left you in the truck, Donny. The crane had a problem and a bundle of steel swung into the back of the truck on your side. It could've sliced through the back window

of the cab and hit you in the head. Jesus, that was close," he said.
"If it hadn't hit the bar in back, it would have been serious." He
shook his head. He handed me a hard hat. I was surprised how
easy he lifted me out of the truck. The tractor didn't have any
seat belts – it was before they were required.

Well, that was exciting. It was a near miss and I didn't
even know it happened. When we completed the loading, we
jumped back into the truck. Dad showed me his itinerary for
the trip to Beaver Falls, Pennsylvania, with stops along the way
to deliver steel to customers he had registered. The sky was
orangey pink as the sun set in the west turning the landscape a
yellowish red that soaked up rays of the sunset. The truck jiggled
along with its headlights on. It was almost dark and would be
another couple of hours before we stopped. I got sleepy. I laid
down on the bench seat. It was cool and comfortable. Soon I
was sleeping.

When I awakened it was pitch black. The truck had
stopped moving. Dad wasn't inside. I looked around and saw
big rigs parked all around. I sat there for a few minutes trying to
get my bearings. I opened the door and jumped down onto the
graveled parking lot. I moved from behind the truck and looked
around. I spotted a lighted building in the distance behind a few
tractor and trailers parked in front of the building. I thought
that's where Dad had probably gone.

It was a moonless night but it was clear and the stars
were shining. I stubbed the toe of my shoe on something. I
looked down, a thick paved asphalt highway came into focus as
truck lights appeared from down the road. I wasn't sure which
direction the road ran. I back-tracked to be safe and kept my
eye on the headlights to be sure the truck would miss me. It did.
Another truck close behind him whizzed by. The trucks didn't
slow down. I got a little scared. I ran across the road before any
other trucks came by. I entered the painted white building. It

was an all-night restaurant with some drivers inside. I saw Dad and he waved me over to the counter to sit beside him.

"Hi, Dad."

"Well, good morning. Are you ready to eat?" he asked.

"Yup."

Dad motioned to the guy behind the counter and he came over.

"Hi, son. What'll you have?"

I looked at Dad for some guidance. "Well, there's cornflakes, toast, or eggs," Dad said.

I thought a minute, looked up at Dad and asked, "A hamburger with mustard and onions?"

The guy behind the counter, my dad, and three other drivers who sat nearby broke out in laughter. "There you go," one of them said.

"It's three in the morning, son," the guy said. "You sure that's what you want?"

I nodded my head and asked, "Can I have mustard and onions too?"

"Can you make it?" Dad asked the guy.

"Sure, Vern. I can make it for the boy." He grabbed a patty and plopped it on the grill.

Dad looked at me and said, "I shouldn't have left you out there. The road is dark, the trucks go pretty fast. It could have been dangerous. Did you see any trucks when you crossed over the highway? That's two for two, Donny. Shouldn't have left you in the truck both times."

I shrugged. "I didn't see anything, Dad. I just wanted to find you."

The next event was less visible.   It also involved me and Dad. Mom asked him to take me with him to Leo Berg's tractor dealership where Dad had bought the REO. Leo was mayor of Akron at one time and my dad got to know him well. The back-end of Leo's dealership was just across the alley to the left of our house with another large doorway, like the steel warehouse in Youngstown.   I passed the front of his business on Arlington Street many times on my bicycle. He always had different colored tractors out in front with sales flags waving in the breeze.

Dad wanted to see Leo about his tractor. It was just before he began to have some initial but serious reservations about being a broker in the steel business. He may have wanted to see what Leo could do for him, financially, if Dad wanted to sell his tractor back to Leo. We entered the large back door to the dealership just inside. Dad said to sit down on the concrete floor and wait for him to get done talking to Mr. Berg. A large tractor pulled inside the back door just ahead of me. The driver put the tractor in neutral and left the motor running. He pushed a button on the wall, a door came down within a three to five inch gap without fully closing.

I sat there minding my own business and making sure I didn't cause any trouble for Dad. After a little time had gone by, I began to get a headache. My dad had headaches like I get when he was small. They call them migraines. I started to feel warm and uncomfortable.   I began to get a little sick to my stomach. I sat there twisting my head and shoulders.

I looked up and saw Dad. He looked at me and rushed to the door and pushed the button to get the door moving up. He picked me up and ducked under the door.

"Are you okay? Are you okay?"

"I'm okay, just a little headache."

"Donny, lay down over here in the shade." He carried me over and laid me down with his hand under my head. He looked me in the eyes.

"How does your stomach feel?"

"It's feeling better. How did you know?"

He stayed with me until I wanted to get up.

"Did the guy who closed the door see you sitting beside the truck?"

"I think so. Why?"

"You were getting poisoned by carbon monoxide. Let's go see Mom." He smiled and said, "I've got to go see Leo again."

I knew what he meant.

These were the kind of times when you forget all about every spanking, whipping, or cross word your parents ever had done or had spoken to you. It made you feel better and good that they cared for you and your well-being.

Dad didn't have a car payment to worry about. We hadn't had a car since the old Ford Model A engine blew up. Mom didn't mind much, because she didn't know how to drive; she was home-bound in the traditional way families were set up at the time. Women stayed home taking care of the family chores and kids if she was lucky enough to have a husband who worked steadily. Wherever we went all five of us piled into the tractor. It began with the White, and now the REO. Dad always took Mom grocery shopping in the tractor, what a hardship that must have been. One night after visiting Red's family one of my dad's good friends from Red Star, I became nauseous on the way home. Told to wait 'til we get home, it became increasingly clear my stomach wouldn't make it. As much as I tried, it wasn't possible. Oh no, up it came christening Dad's new tractor – Henry's Law. Sympathy aside, I was quite unpopular among my cramped family who had to endure the odorific smell until we got home. And, I thought I talked too much.

We advertised for renters. The newly completed outside staircase ran up the back of the house to the second floor that had been my sister Patty's room. Dad converted her room into a kitchen and they moved downstairs with Patty. My brother and I moved to the attic all too familiar by now, but we were used to the procedure.

The renters, Margaret and Oaty Anderson, moved in and took over the second floor, complete with a new kitchen in my sister's old room. There was only one bathroom in the house. Can you imagine that? Therefore, it was necessary for everyone to share the facility. Things happen, they say. Well, one afternoon I needed to use the bathroom on an urgent basis. Mom said if Margaret was in there, to just go up and wait until she gets out. So, I went to the second floor and sat on the top of the steps adjacent to the bathroom by about eight feet. I bided my time silently with eyes fixed on the door waiting for it to open and trying to ignore the pain that was growing. The bathroom door finally opened and out pranced Margaret in all her glory. Apparently she had taken a bath, didn't know anyone was there, and didn't have a stitch of clothes on. She froze, squealed, and jumped back into the bathroom. It was a first for me – a full view of womanhood. I didn't mind the wait.

Things were going okay on the home front. The steel strike hadn't been authorized as yet, but steel was still slow. The defensive move to take in renters was well timed. Things were moving along slowly, but they were still moving. Things abruptly changed, though, when they did. We heard a thud and crash, glass tinkling on the bricks in front of our house at ten p.m. Dad had parked the REO in front of the house on Talbot, instead of the driveway in the alley. Everyone looked at each other wondering where the noise came from, or if it was from the truck. We ran outside to find a car sticking out the rear of the REO's "fifth wheel." A fifth wheel is the name for large Pac-man shaped metal plate that locks the tractor to the trailer in a big rig. The police came, an ambulance came, and my dad got a ticket. The tractor was illegally parked. A tractor was not permitted to park on a residential street. It didn't matter that the tractor was our "car," our only form of transportation. Dad's insurance didn't cover the accident due to the "illegal" citation, nor did it matter about the condition of the car's driver who was inebriated. That hurt. This was the beginning of our family's plight and return to less than good conditions. Dad's reach for the prized golden ring turned out to be a ring made of rusty carbon steel with several layers of gold spray paint.

My dad and mom's demeanor was trained by the necessity to work hard and harder, if need be. That's what they did. They didn't throw in the towel and scream. They picked up the pieces and started over. It was a heavy financial setback with more to come and stay with them for nearly twenty years.

The next day after the accident, I was sent to Zickafoose's store at the corner of Fifth Avenue to get a pack of cigarettes for Mom. "Zicky," the owner, was interested in the accident.

"I heard about the accident in front of your house last night," he said.

"Yup," I said.

"Anybody hurt?" he asked.

"Don't know," said I.

"What happened?"

Now I had to say more. Going against my better judgement, I told him what I knew. "Some drunk hit my dad's truck. It was just sitting at the curb, they gave my dad a ticket. It's not fair."

Zicky looked at me for a minute.

"Guess not," he said.

I paid for the cigarettes, Lucky Strikes. "See ya," I said.

At home, I told Mom about Zicky's interest.

"What did you say?"

"I told him some drunk hit Dad's truck."

"Oh, Donny, you didn't?"

I shrugged. "He asked, so I told him."

"Donny that was his son that hit the truck."

Dad was around more but when he had gone on a trip, he was gone a little longer waiting for a full load to come back home. We'd sit around in the dark watching television. We had gotten one about the time the REO had showed up. It must have been a family present, or a concession to Mom as part of the deal to get the tractor. To have a TV at that time was a big deal. Only one or two other families on the street had one. In late 1949, the neighborhood kids crowded into the living room of Carolyn Crawford's home to watch wrestling. One-by-one the families on Talbot entered the television age. Gorgeous George and other assorted characters along with midget tag teams cavorted on the screen. The Lone Ranger, Captain Video, and Howdy Doody dominated TV and entertained the population that sought distraction from the cold war, the "Atomic Age" and from paying high movie prices.

The Korean War, labeled as a police action, had begun on June 25, 1950, when North Korea invaded South Korea below the 38th parallel. I spread open the Akron Beacon Journal and read intently about what was happening. Communism entered the world of slingshots, BB guns, and bean shooters. Japs and Germans were easy to understand, communism wasn't, and I wondered if Dad would have to go this time. The Korean conflict didn't help Dad's financial problems as much as the renters did. "Wildcat" strikes began occurring as the truckers banded together to stop freight from moving. I don't remember details, but I recall a real problem it had created between Dad and his friend, Red. During this troubling period one of the wildcats erupted and our parents discussed whether he would join the unauthorized strike and what it would mean regarding his paycheck, and how it would affect their bills if he did or didn't join the strikers.

"We can't afford to do anything that takes time away from driving, Eva."

"What happens if they enlist you to be on the line, you don't and then drive?"

"Well, it's a problem, either way. If I don't support the Teamsters, I'll be a target."

"What kind of a target?"

He shook his head. "Well, I'll be in trouble with the Teamsters. I need to find out more, and I've heard about some drivers getting concrete thrown at their cabs."

"Vern, I don't want to see you get hurt."

It sounded serious to me. I admired Dad's courage. Strikes didn't make any sense. Wars didn't make any sense. Grandpa didn't want to work, but Dad was willing to work even if it meant getting concrete thrown at him or worse. He was thinking about all of the bills piling up and threatening our family with the possibility of going bankrupt as a last resort. So between Mom and Dad there existed a slight protective layer with his continued self-employment as a broker hauling steel. To make matters worse, he was in the middle of a major threat no matter how he chose to handle the problem, work or no work. I didn't know whether he was going to drive or not. He did. And he got reported by one of the union members. His friend from Red Star turned him in.

Red, his nickname due to hair color, was in a group of wildcatters who saw Dad pick up a load and drive out of the gate. When the Teamsters notified Dad, he was beside himself. How could his friend turn him in, when Red knew how bad Dad's situation was? Red tried to call Dad a number of times. Mom always took the phone call and told Red, "Vern isn't home." A number of weeks went by and Mom slowly persuaded Dad to talk with Red.

"Red said he couldn't do anything else, Vern. He's a Christian. You know he can't lie, even for a friend."

Dad shook his head. "Christian or not, he shouldn't have done it. No one was holding a gun and threatening him. We're the ones being threatened."

"He said there was no choice, Vern."

"Friend or no friend, I wouldn't have turned him in."

Mom hugged him. "Just think about it. Red's a good man."

Red showed up at our house to patch things up. Red had courage too; it was like walking into a lion's den. I could see Red's side – it was an obligation to an organization that was supporting both he and Dad as drivers and he couldn't lie. Dad was right, he had bills mounting up and a growing family to support with nothing in the bank, and bill collectors on his heels. They talked it out smoothing over both of their positions, eventually shaking hands when Red left. I was glad, because I liked Red. He took an interest in his family and always joked with my brother and me. Our families remained good friends no matter where we lived until Red passed away, and afterward when Mom and Elinor visited each other.

Grandma Erwin had moved to Niles a few years earlier and married a widower, Glenn McDonald. He had visited Grandma several times on Talbot Avenue. Everyone liked him. He'd hold out a stick of gum and when you went to grasp it, the gum would disappear and you would be holding his finger. We made several trips to Niles, located east of Akron near Youngstown. It seemed like it took forever to get there, but with the new roads built over the years it's within an hour's drive. Other relatives lived in Niles, my mom's sister, Aunt Daisy, and her brother, Uncle Kenny and both of their families. Unbeknown to us, Niles would become our new home in 1952, but for now it was a place for vacations.

When we returned to school at Robinson after summer vacations, we would have to write a paper about what kind of vacation we experienced and what we had done during the summer recess. Then we had to read it in front of the class. I weeded Grandpa's garden, chased chickens, and rode the pigs until I slipped off into the slop. It became clear some kids at school were better off than I was. They had vacations in the West, some to Washington, D.C., and some to Florida. Most of us didn't go anywhere, and the colored kids who didn't know what a vacation was either. The reports were revealing and had a way of putting you in your place. I wondered if the teachers fostered the plan to find out more than they should know.

By the fifth grade I decided to make up a vacation that never happened, since that summer it was my brother's turn to stay with Grandma in Niles. It

*Bob, Don, Patty,
Grandma, Linda*

was a proper vacation. The teacher paid more attention to me because of the story I had told. Impressions do count, it seemed.

Even the kids in fifth grade were more responsive to me and more wanted to be friends, some I'd always had trouble with for something or other. The colored kids seemed less responsive, thinking I may not want to associate with them anymore.   I guess it is one thing to include some exaggeration, but another to make something up entirely out of your imagination and pretend it to be true. These kind of things would get you into trouble with the law and there was plenty of that kind of talk that put people in jail, pretending to be a person they weren't in order to receive special treatment. I didn't want special treatment, I only did it out of boredom and saying the same thing year-after-year about a vacation at Grandma's house and the pigs.

One of my friends, Billy, a colored boy whose home I'd been to since third grade, sidled up to me at recess and asked, "Did you really do all that stuff you said?" Now I was in trouble.

"Well, you ever said something you wish you didn't?" I asked him.

"Yeah, I did," he said.

"I didn't do any of that stuff. I just made it up," I said.

Billy smiled, "I thought so. It sounded real fun. I liked it."

"Yeah, I did too"

At the end of fifth grade I turned eleven in June and shortly thereafter, we spent a weekend at Grandma's house. Our cousins, Duane and Billy Granger, told us about a swimming hole nearby. Off we went with some other boys including a boy from New York, who was staying at his grandmother's house that summer. The "hole" was exactly that, a gravel pit created by earth moving equipment. It was abandoned and filled with spring water. It was a great adventure after being covered with yellow-beige colored road dust kicked up from cars running up and down the road in front of Grandma's house on Belmont Avenue extension.

We all jumped in. It didn't matter what swimming attire you wore. Some splashed about in underwear, some jeans, and some didn't have anything on. Neither my brother, nor I could swim and it soon became obvious.

I crept out onto the edge of the slippery clay in water up to my shoulders, near a drop-off someone had found. Warnings of the deep part, the drop-off, were fresh in mind. I lost my footing. Out and down I went, into the deep part. Up again. Air, struggling to regain the ledge from whence I came. Down. The gurgling panic to survive echoed in my ears. Up. I yelled.

Everyone thought I was acting. Everyone except my brother. Down again. My life in slow motion, stop-action picture frames flashed in my eyes. I saw my brother reaching, stretching, and straining to reach out his hand to me:

Life Clasp

I came into this world to dwell not long. Eleven years befell my lot. Except for Brother, my brother, finger tips extended, body and arm a watery precipice to hold; clinging toes dug in; a murky, slippery, water filled pit. My grave had been made ready.

Down once, twice, three times. Flip, flip, flip, event frames; a young life in sequence, instantly and yet forever, slow motion in split-second time. An unknown death sentence reeled off in the dark theater of mind, picture-by-picture for me alone, amid the choking, struggle for air, survival.

Bubbles echoed silly, submarine sounds boiling astride a flailing body. Aware of two worlds, the real, the unlocked vignettes, times past. Frightful, horror-filled, yet peaceful, acceptable at once. Distracting but not distracted, an instinct to survive.

Brother the hero, dragging I the salvaged, gingerly, lest the life clasp break its ties. Finger-tip to finger-tip he pulled. The flip pictures ceased. The air filled, then the sputtering, coughing, tossing back of death filled lungs to its watery owner. The breathing, borne back by sinew, back into the world of living again.

Now, Bobby was a bona-fide hero. Again no one knew. We didn't tell Mom, or anyone else at Grandma's. We didn't want them to know, since they wouldn't let us go to the swimming hole again. Besides, we weren't supposed to be there. Who knows what trouble there would have been if we told. Again, Bobby didn't get his deserved hero acclaim, and a "whippin" was avoided.

Mom didn't know about her boys' nearly fatal experience, and I don't know whether or not we ever told her. The incident, however, is still crystal clear to me. It was June 1951. The sound of the bubbles still echo.

And, I thought I talked too much.

April 1952 to 1958

In the first half of 1952 about May, Dad lost his brand new red REO tractor and flatbed trailer he used to haul steel. Repossessed was the legal basis for taking away his only means of making a living, unless he would be able to get another job at a freight hauling company. The steel strike and recovery period were just too long, and the payments too steep.

Before Robinson Grade School closed for the summer, we made several trips to Niles, Ohio, visiting my mom's relatives, Aunt Daisy, Uncle Kenny, and Grandma Erwin, now newly named Grandma McDonald, after having married Glenn McDonald in Cincinnati, Ohio, in 1950. Making several trips in a short time span was clue number one. The grown-ups were discussing things over coffee more than usual. That should have been clue number two. Brother and I had no idea what planning was taking place; Patty, our sister was only five years old. After the discouraging re-possession, Dad immediately began looking for a truck driving job in Akron when his REO was taken away from the house on Talbot Avenue. We were also making stops at trucking companies in the Niles, Warren, and Youngstown area on some of our trips to Niles. As Dad looked for a job, it became clear what was going to happen. A little later we were told our house would be sold and we would be moving. A real estate "For Sale" sign was placed in our small front yard.

During the summer of 1952, our "mansion" in Akron sold and we moved to Niles. Dad had been hired by Sam Gordon Steel Hauling Company a few days after he had interviewed on a rainy night, while Mom and his three kids waited for him in the company parking lot, watching rain water form rivulets running down the sides of the "borrowed" car's windows. Things seemed to be improving and the prospect of making a move wasn't all bad.

We packed our household goods, left our friends and Henry relatives in Akron and moved most of our belongings to the home on Seneca Street of Mom's older sister Daisy, her husband Bill Granger, and our two cousins Duane and Billy. Their older brother, Dean, had been in Korea serving with the Marines over the last two years. Dean was easy going, funny, and nineteen when he joined the Marines in 1950.

Our furniture was stored in Aunt Daisy's living room and dining room. After completing the move we retreated to temporary living conditions in a small mobile home, called a "trailer" then. The trailer, owned by Uncle Kenny, was located on Grandpa McDonald's property where he and Grandma lived. It was temporary because Uncle Bill and Aunt Daisy were self-building a smaller new house on Belmont Avenue one lot over, adjacent to Grandma McDonald's house. When the Grangers were able to move out of their house into the under-construction new house, we planned to rent their home on Seneca Street. We were settled. The move to Niles, Ohio, finished with big sighs from all of us. Beginning in September we walked a long way to school.

Fortunately, things progressed quickly at the Granger new home site so much so, that they were able to move in to the nearly completed house early, before the heavy snow fell in late November. It was a much shorter walk to Washington Junior High School from the house on Seneca Street. Brother started the eighth grade and I began the seventh grade. At the end of the mid-year grading period the teachers told Mom, "Your boys are very bright."

I was twelve years old and had been hired as a paper boy for "The Niles Daily Times," in January 1953. It was freezing cold. Snow was four to five inches deep covering everything. Christmas was over and the incumbent "newspaper boy" had been scheduled to meet me after school at a pre-designated corner. I was promised by the route manager the boy would walk the route to help me become familiar with the best way to navigate the streets according to the boundaries of the route.

You guessed it, the dad-blamed kid didn't show up after waiting for him for over an hour. At five-thirty p.m., I called the route manager from the drug store on the corner. He said the kid wasn't going to be there, but said, he'd meet me in person and give me the collection book and a piece of paper with directions. I told him okay, but I told myself, "I'm going to remember this; someone lied." After meeting the route manager, stumbling through the snow in the dark with two bags of newspapers on my shoulders and making a lot of wrong turns, I finished the route before the drugstore closed. A few customers opened their doors and handed me overdue payments in exchange for their newspapers. I bought a bag of cookies, sat down on a fire plug and ate the whole bag, shivering, still mad at the first day's frustration on the job. "What was this?"

I realized the route had an identifiable cross-section of the financial condition of the households under my control. I could hold-off supplying newspapers on credit until they paid me, or I could dispatch a paper now and then until they did, or stop the papers. All methods were employed, but nothing could make up for the shortfall I'd experience on a weekly basis. It wasn't because of the cookie habit I'd dispensed with. No, it was simply not a good route.

One of my seventh grade teachers lived on my route, Mrs. Lapolla. She had a large, one-floor ranch style white house, and a large Kelly green canvas awning above her living room window with a large fancily embroidered white letter "L." The house also featured a well-kept neatly manicured front lawn. It stood out in the high dollar neighborhood part of my route at the top of Robbins Avenue hill. An older relative of hers paid me every Saturday morning. I never mentioned anything about being a student or Mrs. Lapolla's teaching role no matter who answered the door. She taught me about diagraming sentences. It was something I liked to do.

"When you're in a hole and can't get out, stop digging," works for me. So I put a stop to the paper route within three months after beginning. By the time spring rolled around, I had calculated I was at breakeven, at best, with only a few packages of cookies showing up as profit. I met the route manager to go over things. I reminded him in a matter of fact way of the cold snowy night no one came to "show me the ropes." I was done. I wouldn't be there for a street corner meeting even though temperatures had moderated by then. I had taken the route from a loss position to breakeven within three months and hadn't taken any day off walking through rain, snow, mud, and freezing temperatures.

I worked the worst of the season, after Christmas, when the route's generous customers finished handing out one or five dollar bills to their paperboy, only to find out I had a bad route that was not salvageable. I gave it back in the same way I got it. That was my last paper route.

Things were also winding down for Mom and Dad. The job at Sam Gordon Steel Hauling Company wasn't the panacea hoped for due to dwindling steel loads. In April before school ended in Niles, Dad was on the lookout for another job. He found one back in Akron. Roadway Express became the company Dad had heard about and wanted to join. Roadway offered good benefits and a solid record of growth with bid runs – meaning, after a few years of company service a driver could work his way up the seniority ladder to bid for more desirable driving routes, reducing the chances of being called in the middle of the night by a dispatcher. Luckily, another situation presented itself similar to the Granger new house build. Dad's sister, Maxine, and her husband, Pete Markovich, were in the final stages of building a new house on Myersville Road in Springfield Township in Akron. We rented the same house as Maxine's family had rented prior to moving into their new home.

We made the move from Niles back to Akron in June, 1953. I took my new learnings with me: diagramming sentences, self-employment, eye-to-eye diplomacy, and roller skating. Roller skating wasn't very useful even after I had learned how to stand up and skate – at the same time.

When school began in September, the eighth grade students at Springfield Junior High School were separated by alphabet. Mr. Crisp was responsible for the A through H part of the alphabet. One of the first few days, as we were changing classes, I recognized a familiar face. It was my friend, Don Stewart from Robinson Grade School in Akron, the friend who had invited me to a Halloween party at the local Salvation Army Corps in East Akron. What a surprise. We struck up our friendship and I began attending Sunday Church meetings with Don at the Corps on Johnston Street in Akron. I didn't know anyone else at school, as yet, but it didn't take long because I signed up for some of the sports programs that were offered. At that time, my height was an advantage, standing at five foot eight and one-half inches tall, and 135 pounds. I played center on the basketball team, and quarterback on the football team.

Mr. Crisp always admonished me to smile more often. Why did he do that?

Before Mother's Day in 1954, a knock on our front door turned out to be Kenny Mitchell. Kenny was the son of John and Mildred Mitchell who occupied the other half of Grandma Erwin's twinplex on Exchange Street when we lived with her. Kenny's age was spaced between my brother, Bob's age, and my age. We had done a lot of sneaking into the Spicer Theater and getting into mischief together. He found out where we lived because his mother and Grandma McDonald (Erwin) still spoke semi-regularly by phone.

Kenny told us about a Swedish Smorgasbord restaurant in Stow, Ohio, where he was working and near where his family then lived. It sounded good. Better yet, he said they were looking for bus boys for the Mother's Day week. He said the restaurant was well-known for its large smorgasbord featuring everything on their gigantic long oval table that had anything to do with Scandinavian food. They also offered lobster, steak, chicken and other popular main courses.

Duncan Renaldo, who portrayed the "Cisco Kid" in a television series in the 1950s, had been a recent customer at the restaurant. That added to the excitement of possibly getting the job. So, off we went with Kenny to apply at the restaurant. It worked. Bob and I became full time employees after Mother's Day and into the summer.

Transportation became a problem before long. Dad had taught Mom how to drive in early March before her birthday. She had driven us to the restaurant many times and picked us up at quitting time, usually ten o'clock at night. It took a lot of gas. It was an inconvenience for her, and she was expecting a new baby in about six months. Dad was usually gone, driving big rigs long distance with layovers. On occasion, we would drive with him to work at Roadway Express, in order for Mom to be able to use the car when he was gone. I always felt proud of Dad as I watched him step up onto the footboard, open the truck's door and step into a big orange and blue diesel tractor already engaged with a Roadway trailer prepped and running, ready to go. I imagined it was as if he stepped into a fighter plane cockpit, sitting in front of the controls, checking them, gunning the motor and then taking off on a mission for parts unknown.

Bob and I began hitch-hiking our way to Stow, Ohio, about twenty miles away. I don't remember what happened to Bob, maybe different schedules, or accepting a bag-boy job at Acme. I know I continued hitch-hiking without him the rest of the summer, morning and night.

One late afternoon after clocking-out a car load of girls screeched their brakes after passing my thumb on Route 91, the main route north to south from Stow, the direction I was heading. They opened the passenger door and I jumped in. "What kind of luck was this?" I thought to myself. There were five giggling girls in the car counting the driver.

"Where are you headed?" asked the blonde driver, smiling. I think she looked for a response, something like, "Wherever you're going, that's where I'm going."

I didn't oblige, exactly. "Well, right now I'm on my way home just north of Uniontown. Is that on your way?"

The brunette in the back seat jumped in and said, "A couple of us just want to ride around. It doesn't matter much where. You have a girlfriend?"

"Kinda yes, mostly no." I scratched my head wondering why I said that.

Another girl with big brown eyes bent over the seat and said, "Well, then, tell us about the 'mostly no' part."

I started chuckling. My eyes darted from one, to the other one, who was hugging the seat.

Then, the driver spoke up, "So, girls, asking too many personal questions are we?"

"I don't mind," I said. "She moved away to southern Ohio toward Marietta by the Ohio River."

"Oh," a couple of them said, in unison.

Things went silent for a little while except for one of the girls, a younger one, who was quietly humming to herself as her head lightly bounced to some musical beat. She seemed to be thinking about something worthwhile to consider.

"Maybe," the young girl said, "you should stick out your thumb, go past Uniontown, past Canton, and keep going south 'till you reach Marietta and find that girl. That's what you want, isn't it?"

She looked at me as though she had it all figured out. She shrugged her shoulders and held out her hands, palms up.

All the pretty eyes were on me waiting for a response.

"That's a long way to hitch a ride," I said.

It got quiet again. I left the silence alone. I thought about Connie Pedersen.

They were going to turn west on Route 8 and go back to Stow. I got out at a light in Ellet, saying, "Thanks for the ride." I winked at the younger girl, and she smiled.

It was good to start running again in the cool night air down Myersville Road past Killian Road to Route 619 in Uniontown, and back again, to get in shape for football practice starting every August twentieth according to state rules. It didn't matter the time, nine or ten o'clock, or later; the lonely road with an occasional car and the cooling temperature made a perfect venue to pound the pavement, to sweat, and to work the lungs and leg muscles.

David Nicklas and I were walking home from a store in Lakemore one afternoon. At the corner of Raymond Street, we came upon a girl, our age, sitting in a lawn chair in a grassy lot beside her home. She had a pink shawl over her lap. The sun highlighted her blonde hair, cut slightly above the shoulders. David and I waved to her. She smiled brightly returning the wave and seemed so happy we had noticed her. I was taken by her friendliness and smile.

"Who's that," I asked David.

"She's in our class, her name's Marilyn Meller. She's sick. I think it has something to do with a fever."

"Really?" I couldn't recall seeing her in school.

The ninth grade students arrived at Springfield Township High School as it opened for the new school year in the fall of 1954. I hadn't thought much about the girl with the shawl over her lap, but wondered why she was sick.

Football practice after school and games on Saturday morning took up most of my time.

A few ninth grade players joined with the Varsity Team in a scrimmage practice game with Uniontown as the opponent. It was a game situation with referees to get everyone ready for the regular season schedule. I played defensive left halfback tackling bigger Uniontown players but, that wasn't the problem. The problem was their offensive right end. He was about six feet three and I had covered him on several prior pass plays, no problem. But on the next running play, I moved into position to tackle their fullback and the tall end snuck up on my unguarded left side. He threw his elbow into the bridge of my nose. I reacted to the blow as I heard a cracking sound. I watched him run away. Blood gushed from my nose. I instinctively cupped my hands to catch the blood trying to keep it from spilling on the grass.

We didn't have face guards that would have deflected the blow. Face guards didn't come as standard equipment on the Spartan helmets until the following year. A referee ushered me to the sidelines. My hands were still cupped, catching the flowing blood.

Butch Daum, line coach, asked, "What are you doing with the blood?"

"I didn't want it to spill on the field," I said.

"Oh. Well, just dump it out," he winced. Looking at my nose, "It's broken," he said.

I let the blood spill. At least the blood dumped on the sidelines and not the field. No one would get smeared blood on themselves or on their uniforms. I was sent to Dr. Lehman in Mogadore, the team doctor for Mogadore High School, to evaluate the damage. He concluded my nose was broken, cracked with a deviated septum. He proposed to reset the bridge and thought he could make it straight again. When head coach Pastuck asked me what I wanted to do, it made sense to me to wait until football was over in my senior year to have it reset. He said if you change your mind, we can have the doctor fix it at any time. That's the way it has been for about seventy years now. With this kind of break, breathing problems develop.

After determining what to do about it, a clear, one-half inch thick acrylic face shield covering the lower half of my face and over the bridge of my nose was attached to my helmet. It reminded me of an abbreviated version of a clear Darth Vader helmet, kind of scary and it probably made me look a lot tougher to our ninth grade opponents as I called out signals at quarterback. The swelling subsided. My nose was less straight, curved a little off-center, not bad but not right, not perfect.

In November before Thanksgiving, I was seated at one of the long tables in the cafeteria used for study hall. Classes were changing and through a set of double doors three girls walked in. Who's that? I asked myself. I watched a trim, pretty girl with blonde hair and bobby sox talking with the other girls. I knew the other two girls, but not the trim one. Wait a minute, that smile, that pleasant look – oh, I think that's the girl on the corner who was sick. I nudged another friend from Lakemore, Johnny Morgan, who lived beside David Nicklas,

"Johnny, who's that with the blonde hair," I asked, pointing to the three girls almost at the other end of the cafeteria.

"The middle one?" he pointed.

"Yes," I said.

"That's Marilyn Meller, she lives around the corner on Raymond Street."

I watched her leave through the opposite double doors. I wanted to meet her. Johnny said something, but I didn't hear him.

"I'm sorry, what?" I asked.

"I thought you knew her," Johnny said. "She got well enough to come back to school just this week."

"I saw her once, a while ago. Just this week, huh?" I repeated. Johnny nodded, wondering why I was so interested. Marilyn Meller, bright smile and pleasant was on my mind. I thought, Connie who?

Several weeks passed. We became a steady couple at fourteen years of age before Christmas that year. Marilyn remembers someone calling her to say they found out I liked her. After a lot of phone calls that's how it all got started in November of 1954. After being seated in a study hall and spotting three girls walking through the cafeteria doors, one whom I didn't know, but who would become married to me for sixty-three years and counting. Time flies.

Everything had gone smoothly in our relationship for seven months. We went to school dances together, either the back seat of an older high school couples' car who drove, or with my mother who, again, offered to transport us when we were left without a ride. Fortunately, there weren't many dances where my mom had to chauffeur us to the school.

By April or May, before school was out for the summer, Marilyn decided she wanted to be free. She was young and she felt tied down. Why go steady through high school without dating anyone else but me? Must have been an unexciting outlook for her. For me, I wasn't looking for excitement, just being with the person I felt so good to be around was enough to hold my interest and attention. So, that was it. Maybe it was my nose.

After talking with her mother, Bea, and asking what she thought, hoping she was on my side of things, her final quotes I remember, "To be or not to be, that is the question," and "Whatever will be will be." It was a popular song in the 1950s, by Doris Day. Well, that didn't give me much hope. So, when we were getting onto school buses one day to go home, I asked her sister, Jackie, who was in the senior class, what she thought. I don't remember what she said. All I can remember was her regretful smile that things hadn't worked out. Bright days became less bright.

The only good thing about breaking up was I, too, was free to pursue things I wanted to do, without the planning and negotiation with a partner who's interest and consideration is part of your daily life's activity. Now it was possible to attend any party, talk with any girl, and be with my friends anytime and anywhere. Well, that sounds good, but doesn't alleviate all the brooding and moping around until time has a way of brightening your outlook on things. Déjà vu – this was Connie Pederson, all over again at about the same time of year, one year later. I was gaining experience in handling a deflated ego in sad situations, when it came to losing a girlfriend.

That summer I worked at the Salvation Army as a handyman doing maintenance, and odd jobs, things like replacing a dented grill on the Army's new Ford Wagon, installing a basketball pole support for a backboard hoop for a playground, repairing a screen door, mowing the lawn, and miscellaneous things. Captain Rice and his wife, had hired me to keep me from working at the Smorgasbord, especially on Sunday, and to become more involved in the Army's programs. He had studied architecture in college, humorous, a good guy and would pick me up for work.

Football practice started up again on August twentieth, as usual. I had begun running at night to get in shape. It was about ten o'clock at night. A car load of girls screeched their tires (again?) after the headlights passed me from behind. The passenger door flew open and a female jumped out and shouted.

"Hey, want a ride, handsome?"

Maybe it wasn't my nose.

I couldn't see who it was, at first. As I got closer, I thought it was a familiar face. It was my brother Bob's last girlfriend.

"Hey, Ann Campbell, what are you doing out here?" I said, as she came into focus. I saw Janet Snyder behind the steering wheel, driving.

"We're just riding around picking up guys," Ann said, laughing, with her hand slightly covering her mouth, as the others joined in laughing.

"Come on, get in," Janet said, motioning her head to the left.

"Oh man, I'm soaked. I can't get in there with all of you. You'll regret it, for sure." I said, shaking my head.

"What are you doing out here, Don?" Janet asked, playfully mocking my own question.

"Getting in shape for football," I said.

"Are you sure you don't want a ride home?" Someone in back asked.

"Positive," I said. "Thanks, though."

"Okay, then. Have a good run. Go Spartans!" Ann directed the chorus of cheers as they sped off down Myersville Road.

I didn't want any of them to have any lasting thoughts of my stinking "T" shirt, as bad it was, and would have been remembered by them. So, the invitation was turned down. I thanked them, again, and starting running behind their car watching the tail lights dim in the distance.

The upcoming football season would be one for my personal record book as well as for my brother, Bob's record book.

The 1955 fall football season was a year in which the Springfield Spartan offensive line averaged two hundred and fifty-five pounds, a truly formidable group of seasoned high school linemen, who would shake the confidence of our Metro League opponents down to their socks. Our line had outweighed, on average, the other teams by fifty pounds per man. The opponents could be pushed around easily, couldn't they? Our team was bound for a Metro League Championship season, wasn't it? Sadly, no. We lost four of the last five games. But, what, then, are these records for Bob Henry, the quarterback, and Don Henry, defensive halfback, who were on the starting team?

Coventry was a tough team from the Portage Lakes area of south Akron. They were always high up on the list of winners in the Metro League in Akron. It was the Spartan's third game of the season. We had beaten North Canton and Kent Roosevelt, no losses as yet. The game was at home in Springfield's stadium in front of the high school running along Canton Road, also known as Route 8. The weather was good, the September evening was cool and the fans were cheering. Coventry was going to be challenge for our linemen, a good contest.

Shortly before halftime, the score was tied at 0 to 0. Bob took the snap from center and ran down the line, made a fake handoff to the right halfback, who smashed into a defensive tackle. He then saw the defensive end juke to the right outside of the scrimmage line; Bob had the option to keep the ball. He wheeled left at a 90 degree angle past the end who was out of position for a tackle, then up the field into Coventry's defensive backfield. The defensive half dove at Bob's churning legs, but failed to make good contact. Bob was running full steam, just out in front of the safety when the safety got cut down by a Spartan end, who was tearing across the field chasing the play. Bob was free, now alone in Coventry's secondary chugging like a locomotive, cheeks were puffing, grabbing all the air his lungs could handle, blowing in and out, allowing his engine to run at super top speed all the way to the goal line. He made it. He made an exciting seventy yard touchdown! Bob's personal best and set a new record. It had been a long time before anyone had seen such a dramatically well executed touchdown running play by a quarterback. The crowd rose to their feet. Bob jogged back to cheering teammates and his acclaim.

As things go, you always have to be looking over your shoulder. That's the way things had gone for Coventry with the final score, as Springfield won on Bob's lone touchdown, 7 to 0.

My record? Well, it's less exciting, more personal. I was sitting in either American History or English class when our head football coach, Russ Pastuck, sat down at an empty desk in front of me. It was an odd thing, this coach entering a classroom to talk with a player while the teacher carried on with the day's instruction.

He greeted me and said, "I want to talk with you about a change."

"Okay," I said, puzzled and wondering .

"You're our defensive half, also the quarterback on our reserve team, right?" he asked.

"Yes," I said, shrugging my shoulders.

"Well," he said, "I want to start you at quarterback this Friday when we play Stow."

That was quite a shock, totally unexpected. I didn't know of anyone who had ever started at quarterback as a sophomore at Springfield. I had never heard of it in my limited experience. So, not only was it a surprise, it was tugging at my loyalty for my brother, Bob, the person who had saved my life only a few years ago. Really, four years ago when I was only eleven years old. Russ jostled, waiting for a response from me. It was hard to think.

"Bob's my brother," is all I could say.

"I know," he said.

"I don't think I can do that," I said, shaking my head.

Russ probably thought he'd never hear me say I couldn't or wouldn't accept such an offer to move into the role as Springfield High School's starting quarterback. Now, he was the one who looked surprised.

"Well, I want you to think about it," he said, and left.

Wow, what a thing to have happened. The coach wasn't done with me yet and I was left with a hard or worse than hard choice to think about. That Friday night we beat Stow 27 to 0.

I never asked coach Pastuck why he was making the change. It never occurred to me that it mattered, but that was the issue, because Bob wouldn't just let it drop without knowing what it was about or why. As it turned out things happened in a way Bob and I least expected.

We played Wadsworth the next Friday night and lost 13 to 14. Our record now, four and one, with four more tough games ahead and outcomes in doubt. I think our coach was totally discouraged with high expectations from our huge linemen and from the experience level of our backs. He was looking to the future. He hadn't given up on the team, but as a coach with his experience, and "Coach of the Year" label, he knew that putting all of his eggs into one year's basket wouldn't extricate him from future losses. He had to plan ahead and develop players on an on-going basis. That's why I think he wanted to make the change and that's where I came in.

The following Monday after the Wadsworth game, Russ again walked into the same class, sat in the same seat. He was also present on Saturday morning for my reserve game.

"I'm not going to ask you if you are going to accept. I'm saying you are starting at quarterback for the Ellet game, this Saturday," he said, affirming his position.

I nodded.

"It's a day game," he said. "I'll see you tomorrow and go over a few things."

I nodded, again. "What about Bob? What will he be doing?" I asked.

"I've got him scheduled to interchange at fullback with Beltz. He'll stay at linebacker. I think everything will work out.

I want you to concentrate on the plays and work hard for us at quarterback. Okay?"

"Okay," I said. I didn't know, my "okay" was securing a future financial grant from The University of Akron where I would be awarded another chance at quarterback. But that's another story.

Russ Pastuck never allowed me make the decision. He saved me from having to make a hard choice. He told me I was going to do it and he never told Bob why. He never told me, either. Two years later in my senior year we were co-champions of the Akron Metro League.

In December, the Henry family welcomed another member, Nancy Carol Henry, born on December 12, 1954. This event balanced the family with two boys and two girls. It had been seven years since Patty was born. Now things changed, everything changed, changed, and changed – diapers that is.

Mom had a lot of work to do, but no hot water hadn't changed. She had to heat buckets of water on the electric stove and carry the hot water down stairs to the basement where our wringer washer was located. She had to lift the heavy buckets for the washing water, and then for the rinse water stored in a tub, then heave the waste water into a high sink draining into a septic system. She quietly accepted the additional work along with all of the other things needing done.

It wasn't an easy life. She had a family of six to care for, preparing meals, washing, ironing, shopping and she did it with grace and without any complaints putting aside how sick or bad she felt at times. Sometimes we become so wrapped up in our own lives we don't take the time to show appreciation, or give well-deserved consideration to those who bend over backward for those they love. Bob and I helped when we were home; it wasn't very often.

Now it was basketball, track, and then baseball that would be attracting our attention. For many students studies took second place to the more interesting extracurricular activities.

But there was something else afoot. And my brand new sister, Nancy Carol, would play an important part of a rekindled relationship with my ex-girlfriend, Marilyn Meller. At the end of last summer after the carload of girls driven by Janet Snyder offered to give me a ride, I was told by someone that Marilyn would be transferring to Uniontown High School.

Before the freshman year began her family had moved from Lakemore to a different home, located on the edge of the boundary for the Uniontown district. So, for the whole time she had been in the ninth grade at Springfield, she and her sister, Jackie, were not allowed technically to be attending Springfield High.

I was sad to see her leave. I felt a need to call her and to acknowledge, at least, that she would not be around school anymore. Having arrived two months late for the start of ninth grade because of sickness known to be rheumatic fever, and now, not being able to attend high school with her friends anymore from first grade on up was saddening. So, I dialed her phone number hoping she'd answer the phone.

"Hi," I said. "This is Don Henry."

"Oh, hi." she said quickly, almost as if she was glad I had called.

"I'm sorry to hear you won't be at Springfield and you're transferring to Uniontown," I quickly got to the point.

"Well, thanks, but that's been changed. It's been worked out."

She told me how the problem developed. She had gone to school to change her lunch period schedule, from the second lunch break to the first period lunch break, when all of her friends were scheduled. Mr. Stone, the Principal, told her she and Jackie shouldn't have been permitted to attend Springfield since they now lived in Uniontown district. She would have to register at Uniontown for the Fall Semester. When her father heard about the story, he went to the school and advised Mr. Stone that he had retained the house he owned in Lakemore as his legal address, even though it was rented to others. Mr. Meller didn't believe there would be a problem. Apparently, the question of the district boundary didn't matter. Mr. Stone agreed, and changed Marilyn's lunch period as she had wanted. The crisis was over.

We had a good talk and I felt she appreciated the call. Nothing was said about getting together, but it seemed as if we were on very good terms. Very good terms.

We dated others that fall, but nothing long term had been established for either of us. At some point after Nancy had been born on December 12, someone got the bright idea if Marilyn was told a new girl had entered my life, namely Nancy Carol, it might cause her to be jealous and that could bring us back together again. The set-up began with a phone call received by my friend, Don Stewart, inviting us to play pool at Patty Plaster's house on a weekend afternoon in late December.

We went to Patty's basement. I was surprised to see Marilyn there. Well, that seemed strange. I don't remember if I knew Marilyn would be there, or not. I don't know who was best at shooting pool. But, Marilyn had my full attention again. I do remember that.

After we left it didn't matter who had set up the pool game ruse, Don Stewart or Patty Plaster, but it worked. Marilyn and I hit it off well. It was the start of the road back to each other. I later asked Marilyn if she would go to the school's spring dance with me. She didn't say no, or find an excuse for not being able to go. From that time on, we have been inseparable.

Nancy Carol, my youngest sister, can take a large part of the credit for getting us back together, even if she was newly born and didn't know much about anything. Of course, Russ Pastuck deserves some credit. It didn't hurt that I became the starting quarterback in my sophomore year. And, lastly, thanks to the girls I dated who remained friends – we just didn't achieve a good enough chemistry level for a long term relationship. It turned into a good thing.

My political career got a boost at the beginning of our freshman year when I was elected to Student Council, and again, during my sophomore year when I served as Vice President. I was elected President of our Junior Class, and as President of our Senior Class. In the last year of High School I was co-captain of our Football team and presented with a trophy by a vote of the teachers and coaches for the "Manhood Award" at the graduation ceremony. So, what propelled me into these popularity based positions? I had worked at becoming more gregarious, outgoing, and smiling a lot more than I ever had before. Name recognition counted for a lot. I joined more school clubs, activities, tried out and secured a position in the school play.

Without realizing it, I was doing something I didn't really like. Smiling wasn't my thing.

Standing around smiling seemed insincere, hard to do, and made me feel like saying, "Let me out of here." I liked having fun and laughing, instant reaction type of things, but smiling all the time wasn't natural for me. I learned from these things that smiling "worked," being social "worked," but for me it was hard work. For some, like Marilyn, it was a natural thing to do.

I had streaks that surfaced when seeing something that struck me as being humorous. One time Bob, Jim Justice, and I were in a car turning from Krumroy Road onto Myersville Road when just ahead of us we saw a tall teenager walking on the right side of the road's shoulder, facing us. As we passed him we all saw the way his clothes fit. The sleeves of his shirt and coat were quite short above his wrists. His pant legs followed in the same manner, about five or six inches above his shoes exposing his bare legs above the top of his socks. The shrinkage couldn't be missed. He resembled a scarecrow, in some fashion, due to his tall, thin, gangly frame.

In an instant, I summed it up.

"Boy, he sure grew a lot since he got up this morning." We all burst with laughter.

Other things wouldn't have fit either on that day. They were "hand me downs." Some of us have been there.

Then there was "the car."

In early 1958 of our senior year at Springfied High, I spotted a '51 Ford coupe, painted with flat black primer. It looked cool with fender skirts over the rear wheels. It sat in the middle of the cul-de-sac at the end of our long street. Our next door neighbor's son owned the car. It had a "For Sale" sign in a back window.

As I arrived home on the school bus each day, there it sat. It hadn't sold for a while, probably because there wasn't any traffic in or out of the secluded dead end street, except for other neighbors who apparently hadn't been interested in the car.

One weekend I decided to take a close look at the body, tires, and inside features. The more I looked at it, the more I began to think about what it would take to own the car and maintain it. I had money saved from working at the Crawford Bindery and hoped it would last until I starting working again at the end of May.

I called the number on the sign and the son answered. He quoted me a figure I couldn't believe, "Forty dollars and it's yours," was the price. We went for a drive in the eight cylinder, stick shift, '51 cool Ford. It seemed okay to me. The engine was loud, the muffler was okay, while not a "Thrush" it had a cool sound. It was a cool car.

"I'll take it." My first car hit the road the last semester of high school. It had a lot of use by Marilyn and me. We would go out at night after school just driving alone together. Up until then, we had to be working out plans on how we were to get somewhere and when we had to leave, according to someone else's schedule. Now, we could come and go together anytime we wanted. It gave us freedom. Now we could "See the USA in your Chevrolet," as Dinah Shore would sing in the Chevrolet commercial on television, or at least we could see our part of the USA in our Ford today or on any other day. It was a joy to have and we never got tired of just driving around together.

The joy began to wane when the first sign of car trouble began. I was steering around a corner on my right, when I noticed the wheels didn't turn as sharply as they should. Then at the next corner it seemed to be okay. Okay, so I parked it overnight.

The next morning it began to act up again. It got progressively worse as I drove. Good thing it was the weekend. I took the car home and pulled in the driveway and kept turning the steering wheel, but the black primer cool car wouldn't turn. It just went straight ahead. I looked over at the neighbor's house. The son's car was gone. I crawled underneath the car and looked at the steering assembly with a flashlight. During the inspection I could see where the steering column was attached to the tie rod framing and front wheel support system. I looked closer and saw a thin, shiny piece of metal bent to form a cotter pin which held some of the weight of the column and kept it in line. With a pair of needle nose plicrs I pulled out the pin. It wasn't a heavy-duty cotter pin. It was a fragile, greasy bobby-pin!

Oh, wow! We were at risk every time we took the cool car on the road. The pin had partially sheared and was ready to fall off. What a way to sell a car to unsuspecting people. I couldn't wait until the son got home. When he finally came home I told him about the problem, holding the pin eye-high, face-to-face, making sure it sunk in what could have happened. He denied everything. To this day I don't know if he had done it or if it was a previous owner.

Later, in my tenure as owner of the '51 Ford with fender skirts, a different mechanical failure could have created another driving nightmare – a front wheel fell off. But, that's another story. I'm sure you have the picture. We lived through it.

August 1958 to September 1964

During the summer of 1958, I made a couple of trips to talk with the coaches at Heidelberg University in Tiffin, Ohio, about two hours of driving time, and to talk with The University of Akron coaches a few miles from Springfield Township, Ohio. The reason for the visits – interviews for potential financial grants to play football at the university level.

The prospect of receiving a free tuition paid grant from either institution was very welcome, otherwise, I would have to find a job to pay for tuition if I chose to go to college. Neither of the grants would include books, but Heidelberg included full tuition and a no cost dormitory and meals, provided I worked about ten hours a week in the cafeteria part-time and for other locations after football season was over. The University of Akron grant included full tuition and meals during football season with the assumption I would be commuting from home without any need for a dormitory. There would be no work requirement in the football off-season.

Russ Pastuck was solely responsible for promoting me for the in-person interviews with each school, arranging interview dates, and giving me football films of any games I wanted to show to the universities' coaching staffs. The rest would be up to me in presenting my abilities based on a review of the films and discussions with them. I would do my best in the show-and- tell interviews.

Bob, who had a car by now and his longtime girlfriend, Marilyn Tressel, volunteered to drive Marilyn, my girlfriend now going on four years, and me for a chauffeured trip to and from Tiffin, Ohio for the interview. So, off we went enjoying the ride, excitement, and the reason for the trip to Heidelberg University.

I thought both interviews, the films, and questions had gone well and covered details of a possible offer and how the grant would be provided. The discussions covered what my responsibilities would include to keep the grant in-force over the complete four years of football and academics at the respective universities. It took a full ten days before I received word. Finally, the letters arrived. I had been accepted and offered grants from both Heidelberg University in Tiffin and The University of Akron to play football at quarterback. All I had to do was accept and sign one of the offers. After the shouting and glee was over, both offers had benefits and deficits that needed to be mulled over. In the end one offer provided everything that made me confident nothing would interfere with obtaining a degree, as things stood at the time.

I signed the offer from The University of Akron.

It would have been good to have gone to a college away from home, experiencing living in a dormitory and taking part in after school activities other than football. A total college experience would have been a plus. But, it would mean long distance from everything else, and with no reliable car, I would have difficulty going to and returning from Akron for various reasons, primarily to be with Marilyn, who by now was more than just another girlfriend. I dispatched the tug of war between the two schools in favor of staying in Akron. The away from home experience could be achieved by renting an apartment in the area around The University of Akron, and accomplished by using money I saved from working summers, and still was, at the Crawford Library Book Bindery in east Akron.

Football practice started in August to get the team ready for the first scheduled game. It was hot and grueling, but not much different from what we had done in high school to get in shape.

The fans were in the stands at the Rubber Bowl in Akron where our home games were played. Among the fans were my Marilyn and Bob with his Marilyn. We were playing Mount Union another university in the Mid-America League. I was at quarterback and a pass play was sent in for the next play. Ray Wiley was playing the wingback position. He also had been awarded a grant from Akron. The two of us from Springfield Township's Metro League Co-Champions were now playing for the Akron Zips.

Something good was about to occur, but I didn't know how good it would become.

"Hut, hut-hut," I barked. Seventy pass play was called in the huddle. Ray brushed the defensive end on his way to a zig-out and then zig-in pattern, some thirty yards downfield to a targeted spot. In the process I had faked to a left halfback diving into the line and dropped back to set up for a pass. There were three intended passing choices, a halfback in the flank, a left end executing a banana left-out, and Ray, about thirty-three yards down field. Ray could catch anything I threw at him in high school. He had my confidence anytime I dropped back to pass.

The Akron linemen executed their assignments, only one defensive lineman was charging me. I let the ball fly. I can still see the arc of the ball as the defensive guy did his best to let me know he was there. He hit me. I hit the turf. But, I saw the arc of the ball.

The pass was on target. Ray's nimble pass-catching hands grabbed it in mid-air, he side stepped one defender, ran with abandon managing to stay clear of any other defender except for one just fifteen yards from the goal line. I still don't know how he did it, but he broke loose from the Mount Union defender, dashed across the goal line for a seventy-three yard touchdown!

Akron's fans, a few minutes before the last play had begun, were chanting, "Rossi, Rossi, Rossi," not Henry, Henry, Henry. Joe Rossi was from Akron Garfield High School where Joe was quarterback. He and Garfield High had a fan base as an Akron city school. Joe's brother, Dom, was a quarterback for Akron a few years earlier, so fans had ample reason to want Rossi in the game. Joe, the other freshman quarterback was vying with me at quarterback. Springfield Township High School wasn't known in the city league, since it was a suburban school outside of Akron. Interestingly, Garfield was our first game of the season for the 1958 Senior Class of Springfield High School. We didn't play our best and Garfield won twenty to six.

The fans dropped their chanting. We kicked the extra point.

The next day, a headline in the sports section of the Akron Beacon Journal read, "Springfield Duo Clicks for 73 Yard Touchdown." What a surprise to see a headline in the paper. And, it was a surprise to see the touchdown set a record for the longest pass play for Akron University for several years to come.

At the football banquet at the end of the year, yet another surprise. I received the longest punt award for the 1958 season. The funny thing is, I had made only one punt that year because the coach let me run the team without sending in plays. It had been fourth down and a long way for first down in our own territory – a must-punt situation. But the regular punter didn't come in to punt. I called for a punt and I did the deed. What a payoff. The punt was about fifty yards, net forty, but good enough to win the longest average distance punt award for the season. It was a good finish for a freshman quarterback, Henry, and for the wingback, Wiley.

The next year would be good in a major way and not so good in another major way.

During the first football season in October, Marilyn and I were talking on the phone. I was in the hallway of the apartment using a free phone. At some point she became silent.

"What are you thinking about?" I asked.

"Just thinking ahead," she said.

"I've been doing that, also. Thinking about when, or what to do about getting married. Last time we talked about it, nothing was decided."

"I know."

"Well, when is the question. Money is the problem."

"What about next year in August?" she asked.

"That's a good time," I said, thinking it wouldn't interfere with football and school starting.

She always has done and still does the thinking for us when something new is about to change things, like renting versus buying a house, location, schools, and then offering suggestions as to how things will work out. This is the same thing she was doing now, before the issue about getting married came up and how we'd go about it. They call it "pro-active."

"I was thinking about August before school begins," she said. "I'm making nearly forty-three dollars a week, net, at Aerospace. That should be enough to get a small apartment."

"That sounds good."

"Doesn't it." She perked up.

"I can probably find a part-time job in January," I said, and then added, "I can give up this apartment to save rent money, go home and save the money. That should help, but it still seems a little bit soon."

"We can make it, I know we can," she said.

I couldn't resist. We both wanted to get married earlier, but we knew it was too soon. This was the right time.

"Okay, then. Go ahead. Put it down on paper and let's take a look."

So things changed. A date for the marriage was set for August 8, 1959. That's the way it happened. It was good. It was major.

The football season ended and I moved back home to save up for the major change. I got an after school job at a landscaping and shrubbery business located in north Akron, and then began working again at the Crawford Library Bindery in east Akron in June.

Marilyn was a beautiful bride. We honeymooned in Niagara Falls on the Canadian side, had room service at the Sheraton Brock Hotel and paid $6.50 for a hamburger. We only ordered one and thought $6.50 was outrageous. In 1958, McDonald's had opened in North Canton, Ohio, selling burgers at 10 cents, fries at 10 cents, and milkshakes at 15 cents for a grand total of 35 cents. Of course, the Sheraton hamburger came with fries and it was the lowest price we could find on the room service menu. I was making 75 cents an hour and Marilyn about a $1.25 an hour at Goodyear Aerospace as a clerk typist. We drove to Niagara Falls in a dark green 1954 Cadillac DeVille. You would think we could afford two hamburgers. Marilyn's dad handed me the keys as he looked at his car, maybe for the last time in such good shape. We finished the weekend trip without a scratch; now back to work for both of us and football a few weeks later.

"Look over your shoulder, something may be sneaking up on you." Good advice.

Marilyn & Don's Wedding

Joe Rossi dropped out of Akron University before the start of our sophomore year, and I had no clue. I was quite interested in another development. Two new quarterbacks showed up, both from Akron schools. One replaced Joe Rossi and an extra guy named Joe Mackey. This new Joe was good, he could scramble, he was big, and he could throw. The other guy nicknamed "Golden Arm" couldn't throw and didn't appear to be nearly as good. But here they were, two new freshmen vying for quarterback. Very interesting.

I looked over my shoulder one day at practice and coming up behind me was Tommy Evans, backfield coach. Tommy approached and put his hand on my shoulder.

"Uh-oh," I thought to myself.

"Don, I'd like to see you in my office after practice and shower. Okay?" he asked.

"Sure," I said.

I knocked on Coach Evans' door and he opened it. "Come on in, have a chair."

"What's up, coach," I replied, without showing my state of mind.

"To be honest and to the point, Don, we have one too many quarterbacks."

I didn't respond waiting for what would come next.

"What we want and hope you'll agree with, is to place you at a position where you can help us and in a position we think you'll do well. We've seen you catch the ball. Laterza thinks you're a natural. What do you think?"

This was an unexpected surprise – I was beginning to like surprises again. I thought I might get cut from the team. Tony Laterza, the end coach, saw me catch every hard ball thrown, meaning up-close ten yard passes from John Stone, the starting senior quarterback, who threw a hard punishing ball. The end coach once asked to look at my hands.

I hated to give up the quarterback position and to get heavily involved in blocking heavy defensive linemen. But, I didn't have any choice. I couldn't negotiate my way out of this "one too many quarterbacks" scenario, but he still hadn't identified the position they thought about.

"What position are you considering?" I asked.

"Wingback," he said.

I nodded. "How does this affect my tuition grant?"

"It doesn't. That stays the same," Tommy said.

"What's the alternative?"

He shook his head, "None," he simply said.

"Okay, then," I said, "When?"

"Now."

I was still on the team. I liked to catch passes. I got up, shook his hand. My quarterback position was left in Tommy's office. I was no longer a quarterback. That position had been a part of me since the eighth grade at Springfield Township Junior High School. This demotion would take some time for the mental adjustment.

This was major. This was not so good.

A couple of things of interest to note, here. We were playing Kent State University in a practice game before the season started at Buchtel Field, Akron University's combined football practice field and baseball field. I was playing wingback and a safety on our defensive team when they had to punt.

It was fourth down for Kent State. The punt was a high, end-over-end arcing ball on the right side of the field. From my position I had to run at full speed to catch it. The ball came up short and took one high bounce, still spinning end-over-end. I believed it would be a line drive bounce into my stomach, instead, the high flying ball was going to be about two and a half feet over my head. I made a reflexive adjustment and caught the ball between both palms while it was still spinning in my hands, end-over-end, without breaking stride. "Soft hands," said Laterza a while ago looking at my hands.

If that wasn't enough for the coaches, I tucked the ball into my side and ran up to the pack of Kent State defenders and made a sharp left cut out of the pack, smashing left and running down the left side of the field toward the goal line. One show-off from Kent State got the angle on me and knocked me down, about five yards out from the goal. "Great catch," and "Great cut, you almost made it," were comments I heard as I ran to the sideline benches.

I sat down on the bench. I glanced at the goal line where I almost got the touchdown and looked at the goalposts. My eyes shifted and focused on the chain-link fence behind the end zone and the short alley-like driveway with sparse weeds growing in the backyards of the houses behind, separated by the driveway. I had a flash-back to a time when Kenny Mitchell and I were peering through the same fence twelve years earlier. It was the same spot behind the fence where we watched a scrimmage taking place and it seemed like a long time ago. We were about seven and eight years old at the time. It was the first time I'd recalled that day in twelve years. It hadn't crossed my mind in all of the practices and scrimmage games that took place last season at Buchtel Field, my first year with Akron University's football team.

Our family had gone back to see Grandma Erwin after we moved to the small house Dad built in Springfield Township. Kenny and I wandered down the alley and crossed a street, still walking in the alley, between the houses to the alley's dead-end that stopped at the chain-link fencing surrounding Buchtel Field. We sat down and hung onto the fence, with our fingers poking through the strong wire fencing.

We watched Akron University's football team practicing. I couldn't believe football was such a fierce game. The action on the field resembled gang warfare. They knocked each other down, grabbed and pulled bodies in all directions, some went flying into the air after a vicious block, while others wrestled each until they both fell to the ground. We could hear the impact of the pads protecting their joints, and the thuds of their bodies hitting each other as the dust rose above the melee. At one point, a running back shot through the line, scored six points and ran under the goal posts in our direction. He pointed at us and gave us a salute.

"I'm never going to play football. They're killing each other!" I said.

Kenny laughed, "Yeah. That's crazy. Doesn't look like fun to me."

How wrong could I be? Here I was, nineteen years old, sitting on a bench in Buchtel Field, allowing nearly grown and fully grown men to beat me up. What irony! What a fun game.

Later on another occasion, coach Laterza and head coach, Joe McMullen were kibitzing at practice as they watched backs and ends run pass patterns with John Stone throwing the passes.

"Okay, Henry. Laterza says you can catch anything. We have a bet. Go down twenty yards go left and catch the next pass Stone throws," coach McMullen directed.

"Banana or cut?" I asked.

"Cut," said Laterza

"Hut," barked Stone.

I took off from an offensive stance down the right sideline and made a ninety degree angle cut to the left. The ball was already on the way as it has to be when passing under real game conditions. I instantly saw the hard thrown ball was in a rising trajectory, much like a hard hit line drive baseball. This was going to no-contest as to whether the ball would be caught or not caught. The ball was out of reach even with a well-timed jump in an effort to catch it.

I watched it fly over my head as I ran underneath the ball that bounced some thirty yards downfield. I didn't even try to jump. I immediately turned to retrieve the ball.

"Henry, get back here," McMullen barked, with feigned disdain.

When I was within earshot, McMullen gruffly yelled, "Why didn't you catch that ball?"

"Why?" I yelled back. It was incredulous. I raised my arm while running back to the group and yelled back to the coach, "It was too damn high."

The backs, ends, and coaches all broke out with laughter, including Stone. It was true. They knew it, but they were primed for a joke and were having fun. I played along.

Obvious things are soaked with humor and that was one I remember well.

I never knew what the coaches' bet was, or who bet against me, but I would bet it was the head coach, Joe McMullen, who bet against me – "too many quarterbacks."

The season ended with, again, more losses than wins. I got in several games but nothing terrific materialized and there are no memorable moments or stellar plays to offset the fact that now I was watching other quarterbacks play and comparing their effort to what would have been my own performance. I made no records or received any awards except for "the most improved back at a new position." It was a new award, one I had made up and given to myself.

I was a married football player. I think others looked at me as if I'd passed some imaginary life point, grown older, and was demoted as a result. At times it seemed it was so, especially at the news Marilyn delivered shortly after Christmas 1959.

"Me, a father?"

"That's right," she said.

It was a moment of disbelief, wonderment at the occasion, and the challenges and responsibilities that lie ahead over the next nine months and beyond. First and foremost, I needed not to be thinking about football anymore, but only about finding a full time job, the sooner the better. I wanted to continue pursuing a college degree of some kind in some way. Marilyn wouldn't be working anymore after the baby arrived in

September, so it would be up to me to provide enough income to satisfy our living expenses and tuition at the same time.

The football grant was good as long as I honored the terms of the agreement, i.e., played football at Akron University and received passing grades. Marilyn and I had agreed when football season began for the 1960 fall season, I would not be able to continue and could not honor the terms of the agreement. I would have to give it up.

Earlier, I had heard about something called the "B Squad" at Goodyear Tire and Rubber Company. The "squad" filled in for regular workers who didn't show up at their job in plants throughout Akron. As I learned more about the possibility, I thought the B Squad could satisfy my first goal of finding a job in the short term. Goodyear provided part-time employment via the B Squad for students who wished to start or continue their college education. If you were lucky enough to be hired into a full time employment position at Goodyear, paid tuition was available provided a passing grade point average would be maintained.

By the end of the first week in January, 1960, I had applied for the B Squad as a factory worker, interviewed the same day, and offered a part-time position seven days later. I started working on January 20, 1960, in Goodyear's Plant 1 on Market Street in Akron, Ohio.

Goodyear fit my work assignments around my school class schedule and over the weekends, including night shifts. What a good deal it was. Fortunately, my grant from Akron University was still in force for the second semester and it would be good until I gave it up. Now, all I had to do was keep my eyes peeled for a full-time position to open for which I was qualified. I needed to get hired by the middle of summer so I could continue my pursuit of a degree, with tuition paid for by the Goodyear Tire and Rubber Company.

This was the plan that we set in motion during the first month of 1960.

Marilyn continued with her duties at Goodyear Aerospace during the regular day time hours, catching a ride from a co-worker and I drove to classes during the day and worked in the rubber factories across an assortment of jobs filling in for regular workers at night.

Work for me was six o'clock at night to twelve midnight, or from twelve a.m. to six a.m. in the morning for others. I fell asleep in class at times and once while taking an economics exam in a morning class. I had answered about five questions before going nite-nite and woke up with fifteen minutes left to answer the next seventy-five questions that included math calculations. Struck with panic, my bloodshot eyes had to work very fast.

During the work area assignments, I would approach the shift manager and inquire whether he was looking to fill any full time jobs. One particular job would always need B Squad help. The job required spraying mold release agents inside open-end "barrel" shaped truck, passenger, and motorcycle tires after lifting them from a moving conveyer hook-line carrying the tire barrels. The open ended barrel tires were carried along on the hook line and taken to the tire molding department where they were placed into large, hot, highly engineered tire molds called "clam shells," due to their appearance. After molding, the tires were sent on to the quality inspection department before final wrapping and shipping.

The spray fumes were acrid and sticky, sinking into your hair and covering your work clothes from chest high down to your shoes. No mask was provided or worn. At the time, I don't think OSHA was involved. There were exhaust systems in the booth, but they didn't work very well. That's why there were so many absentees for that particular job. No one liked it.

The barrels were heavy and four spray machines had to be kept running simultaneously by grabbing a sprayed tire barrel and throwing it onto a return hook and then lift an unsprayed barrel to throw onto the empty mandrel, then flip the switches to start spraying the raw barrel. Back and forth from four machines, from line to line, throwing barrels and switches, in a synchronized choreographed dance swinging to and fro, in time, keeping up with the machines. When the six hour shift bell rang, it was time to be tired, and time for a hot shower.

Well, it paid a high hourly rate, rightly so. I pounced on the opportunity like a young cat, unaware of any pitfalls, only seeing the carrot at the end of the cart, or in this case – a mouse ready for the taking.

"Is there any way I could get the spraying job on a full-time basis?" I asked the manager.

He looked at me, kind of puzzled. "Well, maybe. I'll have to check with the Department Manager and see what he says."

"Thank you."

Later, my B Squad manager, Jim, tacked a note on the cork board, "See me," it said.

It was July. Time was getting short. I'd been working in many places. School was out which meant more time for working with increasing wages. At that time workers were paid in cash and change. I picked up my wage envelope from the B Squad manager and followed up on the tacked note.

"You said you wanted to see me?" I asked, referring to his note on the board.

"I've had several shift managers say that you want a full-time job," he said with a smile.

Uh-oh, I thought. "Yes, I do."

"There are a lot of things that have to happen before someone gets a job in the factory. You do have good reports from your assignments. That's in your favor," he said.

"That's good to hear," I nodded.

"Well, that spray job's not for you. Really bad! But I've got something you might want to look at. How's the wife doing with the little one?" he asked, now becoming cordial.

"She's just fine. Getting anxious, you know. It's been a while," I smiled.

"Our research group on the boulevard has an opening. It's a salaried position as a lab technician. I thought of you. Since you're married and stable, I think you'd be a good fit for the job. Do you want me to let them know you'd like to be considered?" Jim smiled, again. He didn't smile much.

"Yes, absolutely," I said, internally jumping up and down with joy.

"Okay, we'll set it up." He reached out and shook my hand.

By August 10, 1960, I had managed to obtain full time salaried employment as a lab technician at Goodyear Research on Goodyear Boulevard. Yes, it was a Good Year!

Part of our plan was for me to leave Akron University and transfer to Kent State University because of the lower tuition cost. Under the Goodyear plan for paid tuition, I would be responsible for tuition payment up front. After submitting passing grades, I received one hundred percent tuition reimbursement from Goodyear. Okay, where's the problem? We had to take out a bank loan before each semester started in order to cover the tuition and books.

I enrolled at Kent State for the fall quarter.

Before our baby was born, we moved into an apartment in Ellet off of Albrecht Avenue, not far from Meadowridge Road, where my father built our family's first house.

In September on the thirteenth day our first son, Richard, was born with a characteristic grimace and yellow blonde hair. With fists clenched, he squealed with all his might as if to question the whole affair, "What's going on here?"

Well, that changed things for all of us in 1960. And, changes kept coming for the next few weeks, the next several months, and the coming decades. We were off on a quest. Little did we know how long it would last, and what else was in store for us and our little band that was sure to grow in numbers as time moved on.

By the time snow arrived I was tired of the pace. Running to and from Kent State in the morning, off to Goodyear Research by three-thirty p.m., home by twelve forty-five in the morning, I went to bed by two a.m., up at seven a.m., and did it all over again the next day. For what? I had a job.

One day I decided for some good reason to stay home from school. It turned into two days, then three days. Before long, the last time I went to school I cleaned out my locker. I withdrew from classes. It was late 1960, no Goodyear paid tuition was due. We had to pay the bank loan.

During my trips to Kent State I passed a housing development, Dover Homes, in Brimfield. A ranch style brick house could be purchased for $11,995.00 for only $500 down. I saw the billboard every day on the way to school. We became the beneficiary of a $500 windfall during the month of January. With the help of Marilyn's father who co-signed a second mortgage, Marilyn and I purchased that $11,995.00 Dover brick ranch style house in Brimfield. We were able to do with the modest salary I was making at Goodyear Research. I was a college drop out.

In June of 1961, we moved into 35 Ivanhoe Drive in the Dover development. Grass had to be planted, draperies, painting, and flooring needed to be installed. We were busy with making a home and a university education was far from our thoughts. Ricky's first birthday rolled around and his traditional German chocolate cake was in the oven. Our second son, Douglas was also in the oven ready for delivery by January 27, 1962.

I went to work every day at Goodyear Research. There wasn't any reason to dislike the kind of work I was doing. It was interesting and I learned a lot about scientific analysis and methods to obtain testing data. I can't forget the first time I was assigned to learn how to operate a newly installed machine. My knees shook, standing in front of the massive Consolidated 21-101 Mass Spectrometer. Red and green lights were blinking on the control panel with valves and gauges to allow sample gases into the unit to be analyzed. The maze of sequencing steps had to be specific and memorized or the gas sample tube could be emptied, destroying hours of research chemists' work who supplied test samples to our lab. The machine was connected to a punch card computer and an ancillary carbon electrode destructive electric arc furnace to vaporize samples in a millisecond resulting in a bright combustible flash in the test tube – it caused my nerves to quiver. It wasn't boring work since there was an element of doing something wrong and costing time and money if not handled properly.

Well, time passed and I became discontented. I had no way, known to me, to make any forward progress with a higher level position and higher dollars. I was stuck. I felt a need to make a difference if not in dollars and cents, then doing something that mattered. Earlier, when attending the Salvation Army I thought I should become an officer. The thought was in the back of my mind. I had never acted upon it. Other directions had taken precedence. Army people were good people. The role models I had kept in mind were Captain and Mrs. Rice, who we had known at the Johnston Street facility and who I worked for in the summer of 1954.

Without getting into detail, Marilyn and our family found ourselves in the fall of 1963 at the Salvation Army School for Officers Training in the Bronx, New York City, New York. Marilyn was okay with it, as long as it was something I needed to do.

"Anyway," Marilyn's favorite segue, we did it all in cadet's uniforms. We sold the weekly War Cry to anyone who would open their door to us and take an interest in the articles. We walked up and down stairs knocking on apartment doors, holding street corner open air meetings in Greenwich Village, marching on 5th Avenue, and attending classes at training school.

It was busy, but not busy enough. Our third child was soon on the way and, again, totally unexpected. Late July was the expected celebratory date.

Marilyn and I had done well in all of the classes. The school was run like any school would be run and organized with instructors, exams, and deadlines. I was encouraged by the way my mind was working and had received high marks. Scrawled on a paper I had completed was written, "Did you copy this from somewhere?" I hadn't.

At the end of the first school year the cadets, married, or single were handed their assignments and where they would be stationed for the summer. It was late in Marilyn's term, about May, 1964, when we were assigned our location. We were to be located in Jamaica, Queens, New York City for the summer. This was a shock to us. Northeast, Ohio, was the place we wanted to be, near Dr. Walker, a disciplinarian who had delivered our first two children. We hadn't discussed this with the leaders of the school thinking they would know our preference. They hadn't initiated any discussion with us, either. Sort of a Mexican standoff. I was elected president of the class and we were scheduled to be commissioned in the spring of 1965 which weighed on us, but with some deliberation, Marilyn and I decided we didn't want to be stationed in Jamaica.

I advised Colonel Tallmadge in a less than thoughtful dramatic way I regret doing, by tearing up our summer station orders, knocking on his door and handing him the pieces. He looked down at the pieces of paper in his hand.

"What's this?" he asked, totally bewildered.

"We're not going to Jamaica," I instructed.

"Why? We thought you'd want to be with the doctor working with Marilyn," he said.

"No, we wanted her doctor in Akron to deliver our baby."

With that terrible exchange, I turned around and left. Later, reality set in and we decided to retract our decision by staying in New York where our baby would be born. We intended to remain for the full two years and be commissioned officers. On July 30, 1964, our only daughter sweet Vicki Lynne graced the world of New York City with her birth.

We moved into quarters on the second floor of the Jamaica, New York, Salvation Army Corps building in Queens. It wasn't long before we knew we were in the process of making a mistake that only could be corrected by vacating our cadet standing and leave the Army.

Marilyn flew out of New York City on a four engine, triple tail, Lockheed Constellation, one of the sleekest airliners at the time only seven days after Vicki was born. I had done preparatory work and made contact with my last employer Goodyear Research and Howard Nicol, who was Vice President. He told me to stop in and we would talk when I returned to Akron.

Until we found an apartment we stayed with Marilyn's parents for about a month. Marilyn searched and found a basement apartment on Tudor Avenue in Ellet.

Mr. Nicol was quite introspective and quizzed me about the change I had made. In the end, he offered to place me in the radio-active cobalt 60 laboratory. I don't know if he had a background in nuclear radiation, or not. I suspected he may have placed me in the cobalt 60 lab to get my brain fixed by being subjected to a few stray rays of radiation. It must have worked. From that point on, I was driven to get through school and obtain a degree.

I made good at least once in my lifetime at twenty four years of age. I entered The University of Akron night school and received a bachelor's degree and completed all requirements for a master's degree in one year, before leaving Goodyear Research. Mr. Nichol applauded my efforts, and with thanks to him these things were made possible and were completed in good standing.

Goodyear Tire was one of the last paternalistic major corporations I worked for that continued to provide for its employees and their needs in a co-habitation and symbiotic relationship. The company provided its workers with every promise made and looked after their well-being. In return the workers did their jobs well and continued to work for the company into retirement and beyond.

This great relationship between employees and their company lasted for years since its founding by Frank A. Seiberling in 1898, with a loan of $3,500. Seiberling fostered the use of Charles Goodyear's contribution to the rubber industry who had made the discovery of rubber vulcanization. Seiberling was also responsible for the company's trademark name "The Goodyear Tire and Rubber Company," and for the winged foot logo – a symbol of Mercury's speed.

Most people think Goodyear was founded by Charles Goodyear and are surprised to find it's not true. Even though I worked there for several years in the plants and in R&D, I didn't know this fact until I left the company several years later. Goodyear died penniless in 1860, at the age of 59, and didn't realize how his work had secured employment for thousands of dedicated workers and the growth of an industry that most likely has gone far beyond his imagination.

September 1964 to 1977

It was good to be back in Ohio on the campus of Akron University and to be working in the lab for Goodyear Research. It seemed we had lost some things: a new house in Brimfield, about three years of service toward retirement at Goodyear and some lost face for not completing the officer training program for the Salvation Army. The change had to be made.

We both were still only twenty four years of age with a young family and, again, we were working toward an improved life together.

The experience of living in a large metropolis like New York City had afforded us first hand exposure to the gigantic scenes and buildings, Wall Street, the Empire State Building, and Tad's Steak House with huge baked potatoes and, of course, the subway. New York's bigness impressed Marilyn and me, which was the first thought we experienced on our trips to and from the city as we carried out our duties. The next thought was the sardine-like feeling of the crowded city from elevators and subways to sidewalks. For two people who were used to suburban living, uncrowded spaces, with lush foliage between spaces, New York City had really close quarters, some of the sights between spaces weren't as scenic.

The people I'd be working with in the cobalt 60 lab were great people including Patrick Reilly and Hans Widmer, both held PhD degrees in chemistry and nuclear physics. Pat was especially charismatic who enjoyed everything from golf to classical symphonies, to Shakespearian plays in the Cleveland area, as well as just eating a salad for lunch. Marilyn and I visited with Pat and his wife, Catherine, and joined them in variety of the activities. When he attended yacht meetings at Portage Lakes he would wear his captain's hat – he looked every bit the part of a sail boat captain which he was. Sometimes we hurried through nine holes of golf at five-thirty in the morning at Turkey Foot Golf Course and would be at work before eight o'clock to start the day.

Pat as department manager gave me the latitude I needed to be at school for any class that would conflict with my work schedule which initially began at three-thirty in the afternoon to midnight. As I got closer to graduating, I was permitted to work around any work or class conflict that arose. It was a good situation for me and I didn't take advantage of the casual arrangement. I always worked forty hours each week.

Marilyn was busy, of course, managing everything related to our lifestyle, whether it was shopping for groceries while pulling two, or sometimes three grocery carts – three kids in one, groceries in the other – or washing, ironing, and all of the housework. She did it all with a positive attitude and doing her best to be happy knowing at some point in time this would pass. She was a class act and has maintained her optimistic outlook no matter how gray the sky or how bleak some parts of our life seemed to be at the time.

Of course I was busy carrying two lunches which Marilyn packed, one for work and one for school. I left the house at seven-thirty a.m. and didn't get home until twelve-thirty in the morning the next day. Weekends were devoted to studying. In between all of that a funny but morose thing happened one day when our son's first grade teacher called our home phone.

"Mrs. Henry?" the teacher asked.

"Yes," Marilyn replied.

"This is Ricky's teacher. I just wanted to talk with you and ask if everything is okay."

"Why, yes. What's the matter?" Marilyn was startled.

"Well, I was talking with Ricky. He said his dad had died."

"Oh my goodness! No, he hasn't died, he's fine. I'm so sorry," Marilyn replied.

"I'm so glad to hear that. Please forgive me, but I had to call you," the teacher, was relieved nothing had happened. She agreed with Marilyn that it was just a mistake and Ricky would be assured his father was very much still with us.

Marilyn and I figured that he overheard a discussion about the first time I had gone to a dermatologist for eczema. The prognosis: "dried" skin. We believe Ricky heard this and thought I "died." Since I wasn't around much when he was awake, his six year old mind put two and two together and came up with the idea that I was dead. We had a laugh and called the teacher.

So, that was the way things developed over the last two years. I completed requirements for a Bachelor of Arts degree in Secondary Education going full time and back-to-back in two summer sessions ending in August, 1966. Graduation was scheduled for January, 1967. Why wait?

Immediately, I entered the Graduate School program in September, 1966, and finished the 30 hours of study that were required in June, 1967, for a Master of Arts degree in Education with a Business major. I graduated in January and June of the same year certified both as a secondary teacher in English Literature/Accounting, and as a High School Principal and Superintendent for Ohio schools, while working at the lab.

Why wait for that?

Prior to graduating I interviewed with Goodyear Aerospace for an Administrative Engineering position with the Avionics Group at the company located near Derby Downs and Goodyear's Air Dock. All I needed was a copy of a letter stating I had met all of the necessary requirements for a Master's degree in good standing at Akron University and a copy of my 1966 Bachelor's degree. I began working at the Aerospace facility in June, 1967, as an Administrative Engineer passing a level "B" Secret clearance with responsibility for several military contracts.

I also interviewed for a teaching and coaching position with Springfield Township High School and received an offer. Charles Reiger, who at the time was superintendent, made the offer which included teaching bookkeeping and assistant football coach. I just didn't want to become a teacher. I didn't think I'd be happy with the routine. Three months off would have been great and football would have been interesting even if it meant time after school hours. In the end, after reviewing the path I had chosen, a guaranteed pension would have made good sense. Who knows, maybe I would have died from "dried skin" teaching disease, shriveling up my penchant for variety and opportunity.

We moved from the basement apartment on Tudor Avenue to Sarlson Street in Kenmore next door to Ray Wiley and his wife, who were both school teachers after graduating from the University of Akron. They recommended the house that was for rent and it worked out great. Ray and I had a common bond from high school and college with similar outcomes. Ray and his wife, Molly, got married after the second year at Akron University. Ray gave up his football grant in 1960, as I had done, when their firstborn was on the way. He worked in Firestone's retread tire factory while continuing his education. He also graduated with a Master's degree in Education and remained in education rising to a principal level position.

We got together often. We watched the first Super Bowl at his house mainly because he had a color TV which we hadn't purchased as yet.

What happened in this idyllic environment? Same thing as before, same song, different verse.

I hadn't seen Kenny Mitchell since eighth grade in 1954 on Swineheart Road and working at the Smorgasbord in Stow. It had been fourteen years ago. He had located us and phoned ahead and there he was in 1968, standing in our living room on Sarlson in Kenmore. Kenny had already been tapped as an executive at Sears in Chicago's headquarters. It was great to see him. Unfortunately, Kenny was released from his job when financial problems got tough for Sears.

Kenny told us he was now a Baptist Minister in Missouri. He said he was enjoying himself more than he ever had along with his wife and kids. So, as before, he told us about his new job. We talked about the ministry, our time with the Salvation Army, and our East Exchange Street and Spicer Street "gang" until he had to go. That was the last time I saw him.

Bill Stevens and his wife, Rosalie, another couple who were in the School for Officers Training Class of 1965 just like Marilyn and me. They had been commissioned in 1965 and were stationed at the Salvation Army Men's Center in downtown Toledo, Ohio. Marilyn had called Bill's wife to ask for her help with a fashion show at the Johnston Street Army Corps building, the reason why they had come. We enjoyed the time reliving some of the stories we experienced at the training school.

Both of these visits were thought provoking and caused Marilyn and me to review the reasons for the choices we had made over the last eight years. The visits by Kenny and the Stevens' were inspiring. Marilyn and I began to consider why we left the Army and what our future would become.

In March of 1968, we began thinking seriously about the possibility of reapplying for the officer training school and completing the last year in order to become officers in charge of an Army Corps, a legally recognized equivalent of an ordained minister of a church.

That's what we did. We sent a letter to the Commander of the Northeast Ohio Salvation Army asking for assistance in pursuing this latest idea. Shortly afterward we received word that it would not be necessary to complete the final training year in New York City. Further, that we would retain cadet lieutenant status and a need had arisen at the corps in Sandusky, Ohio, for officers in charge. If we were interested in accepting the assignment, they felt we were qualified and would be commissioned with the current class of cadets in New York City in 1969.

In June of 1968, after having spent only one year at Goodyear Aerospace, we were waking up every morning in Sandusky. Several things needed to be done at the corps. Marilyn had responsibility for the women's programs and other activities. We were both engaged in setting up different programs and developing the congregation leadership. It sounds like a lot, but there were only twenty-three to twenty-eight members in regular attendance.

We held street corner open air meetings to bring new people into the meetings. Little by little we raised the number of people attending including some prior members who began to show up. I think by the time the fall season was over we had fifty people in attendance on a regular basis. I started a basketball team with scheduled practices run by a member coach. I also started up a brass band by writing letters to northern Ohio high schools asking for donations of useable brass instruments. We had a great response. I travelled to the schools and picked up free instruments, tubas to coronets, and hauled them away to a couple of rooms at the corps.

In the meantime, our son Rick who was now eight years old that summer had stuffed a box at the Red Barn fast food restaurant for a chance at a "Tin Lizzy." It was a gasoline engine scale replica of a model T Ford sold for entertainment and advertising.

Rick had filled out many entry forms for himself, but only one for his younger brother, Doug. On the day of the drawing, we received a call from Red Barn.

"Hello, Mrs. Henry, this is the manager of the Red Barn.

"Congratulations! Your son, Doug, has won the drawing for the Model T Ford," he said.

"Doug?" she was puzzled.

"Could I speak to Doug, please?" he asked.

The manager talked to Doug and you could see Doug's eyes light up and the biggest grin came over his face. He started jumping up and down. "I won, I won," was all he could say. Doug handed the phone back to Marilyn.

"Yes! Doug won. Will you please give us a call to let us know when you can come to our store; we'll help you get it loaded. Okay?"

"I will. Thank you very much," she said.

You can imagine how thrilled Doug was and how bewildered Rick was. We consoled Rick who thought it should be his prize since he filled out the entry forms. We managed to have the boys accept our idea that there were two owners of the Tin Lizzy. So, both owners could take turns driving up and down the sidewalk on Columbus Avenue, one of the busy streets heading into downtown Sandusky. After several days, maybe a week or two of their sidewalk travels, they were stopped by a man in uniform. The uniformed man was a policeman from the city of Sandusky.

"So, boys, I have to give you a ticket for speeding," the officer smiled.

But, he quickly gave them a lecture about how motor vehicles aren't allowed on city sidewalks. Apparently, some of the neighbors had complained about the noisy lawnmower type of engine running up and down past their houses. Additionally, it was a safety hazard for people sharing a "roadway" with the vehicle who may be hit by the unlicensed drivers, especially the elderly walkers who may have canes and other walking aids.

The boys were scared stiff. They drove home fast to let us know about the policeman who had stopped them. Shortly,

Rick & Doug's Tin Lizzy

the police officer arrived in front of our house. I was outside, but didn't see the officer stop the boys about a hundred yards down the block.

After greeting me he reiterated the concerns the neighbors had and the additional hazard potential of the boys being on the sidewalk. He was very polite and understanding. He also suggested we take the boys to a local schoolyard where there was a track and not that busy during the summer. They could drive without any concerns of neighbors or others getting hurt on the sidewalk.

I assured the officer the sidewalk driving would cease and apologized for being short-sighted. I didn't recognize the problems for the neighbors and the safety concerns that were well founded, especially given how fast the Model T could seem to travel on a narrow sidewalk. I should have been more concerned and diligent in looking after their driving routines and habits. The boys had narrowly escaped a speeding ticket and having their automobile towed with a fine imposed for an illegal vehicle on the sidewalk. But there would be other times, later, when they weren't so lucky, say about eight to ten years later.

Things were progressing well at the corps. Then one cold winter night a gas outage left Sandusky citizens in a state of deep freeze. A gas main ruptured at a sub-station. It was an emergency. My members began calling me asking for space heaters. The stores were all sold out by the time I got there. An emergency and disaster truck was dispatched from Lorain, Ohio, and Captain Reggie Russell popped out of the truck. He had been on the staff at the training school in New York. He was there fully equipped and stocked with doughnuts and coffee. He stuck a microphone up to my mouth and whispered, "We're on the air," and he said, "Say a few words." I did the best I could with the impromptu on-air position in which I found myself. I wondered if I had passed my first live interview as an "acting" Salvation Army Corps Officer. I quickly handed the mike back to Reggie.

Shortly after the outage had been corrected, an executive from Columbia Gas came calling. The gas company wanted to thank the Salvation Army for helping out. The emergency truck that parked at the sub-station handed out sandwiches, coffee, and donuts at the site for their repair team and field workers who solved the emergency situation. It was a reciprocal gesture. He then thanked me for the effort and handed an envelope to me – a check for $2,000 dollars.

While it was still cold in early spring the weather forecast began alerting people to a "Nor'easter."   I think that's what it was called. Sandusky, like Cleveland is perched on Lake Erie, but at the end of its southwestern edge a northern swing in the shoreline takes it to Toledo, Ohio, due south of Detroit. Okay, sounded like a rain storm was approaching the Sandusky area. It didn't raise my excitement level, but rather than stick my head in the sand I felt I needed to do something, but what was I to do? I decided to get in the station wagon about nine-thirty at night and drive around to see if anyone needed help.

I began to see what was going on as the water rose halfway up my wheel covers as judged by the few parked cars and a lonesome driver who passed slowly. Not many cars were out. The streets were deserted and the closer to the lake area I got, the deeper and faster the wind swept rain had become. I began to think I might be the one who has to call for help, or to flag someone down for a ride if I stayed out any longer.

I turned around and headed for home

Later, I had to be out of town for a weekend with my wife south of Columbus, Ohio, for a retreat where I was invited to attend and be one of the speakers. I asked one of the regular members if he would take over in my absence, open and close, run the meetings and be the leader on Sunday morning. The reason I asked this individual was because he was steeped in religion, knew the Bible and was always open to take a role in meetings. He didn't hesitate. I advised Cleveland Headquarters the corps was covered. When we left, I gave him a set of keys. At the meeting on Sunday before I was scheduled to speak, I was advised someone from Sandusky called Headquarters in Cleveland and reported that I wasn't there, and no one else was there to open the doors and run the Corps. Wow, what a shame.

As I drove back from the retreat we passed a number of new housing developments around Columbus. The homes were large two story homes. Suburb subdivision after subdivision surrounded the city, nice homes. I thought about our home. It was on the left side of a duplex, rented by the Salvation Army, a large hole in the living room ceiling hadn't been repaired by the landlord, an older home from the late 1910s with very high ceilings and old appliances and fixtures. Major Atwell, from Headquarters had visited us in Sandusky and provided us with a budget to buy new furniture for the downstairs area that helped. The house and furniture wasn't something we would have had – it would be different – if I would have continued a career with Goodyear, or with other manufacturing companies.

Marilyn was in her fourth month with our fourth child, due in August. I should have a better job, something that could and would raise our standard of living.

I began to think I wasn't cut out to be an officer – something always came up. One year to the day in June, 1969, I decided to give up the plan to finish officer training school.

As a result, I secured a position in June at the B. F. Goodrich Company in Akron, Ohio. I had been hired as a Market Planner in the Industrial Division at the company's headquarters at $11,000 per year. We rented a home in Cuyahoga Falls on the north side of Akron. Rick and Doug would be starting school in the fall and Vicki, five years old, would enter kindergarten.

On August 31, 1969, William Vernon Henry opened his eyes to the world for the first time and got a smack across his buttocks. Welcome to Akron, Billy! Keep your fingers crossed, Bill. We were and still are a band of the "final four," children that is, and six including Mom and Dad.

In the market planning position travelling was part of the job, but not as much as other future positions. I didn't like to travel that much, but it was necessary. The positive aspect of course, was that I was able to see firsthand the sights and sounds of cities I'd only seen in books, movies and pictures. Equally important was taking my turn experiencing walking in the airports, and riding in taxis, hotel vans, traffic, and the rental cars. The hum of the cities and noise of the subways, the cultural and geographical differences, and the everyday accents, that I misjudged on occasion, would become an education in and of themselves.

There were opportunities at BF Goodrich within the other divisions where you could apply for an opening without any negative consequences. What was frowned upon then, was becoming a job-hopper, someone who would go from job to job, company to company, within a relatively short time frame. The reason why you left a job wasn't important, just the fact that you made several moves in a short time was a reason to have your resume pitched into a waste basket. Some hiring managers were not as inflexible and would consider hiring a job-hopper. I was more of a job "wanderer," searching for stability and self-actualization.

I worked in the market planning position for two years, then I moved to the Tire Division as a Product Manager at a 10% increase in salary, which was the going rate.

After being at the Tire Division for a year and with a total of three years at The B.F. Goodrich Company, I felt the need to catch up to my peers in salary due to the detours taken such as dropping out of college for five years and chasing a post with the Salvation Army for another two years, a total of seven years lost in time and money. I needed to hurry. Job-hopping became not only a method of increasing a salary, but sometimes a necessity. It was 1972, and companies were beginning to fire people more frequently due to bottom-line problems. The steel strike and gasoline shortages were looming in the near future. A boss would have to take the easiest and quickest way to reduce costs and that was head-count.

Later it became fashionable to cut factories and that I call "plant-count," closing factories and sending jobs to Mexico and China. Job-hoppers, head-counters, and plant-counters, all have had effect on job stability in the United States – "Paternalism" was finished, over with and done.

I became wrapped up in the game. We took the first step in the process and moved to Iowa, Muscatine to be exact. A quaint little town on the Mississippi River where catfish were big enough to ride. I told our four children about the big fish as if I was Mark Twain spinning a yarn – a story to help them want to make the move. I had seen photos of huge catfish that if caught would have been big enough for them to ride. The tale had some merit. Bandag was the company, cold process retread truck tires was the product. Bandag had revolutionized the retread tire market. Its patented process and growth caused the company to be called, "The darling of Wall Street." But it wasn't a darling in any sense of the word from my viewpoint. The only good thing that came from Bandag was my very good friend and co-worker, Dennis Virag. He supported my job searches, we keep in touch, and our families still visit with each other.

From there we moved to St. Louis for a stint with a steel tubing distributor. What a trip it was. I was slipped my first "mickey," or spiked drink, by a so-called company friend just before hosting a meeting and introducing a steel manufacturing Vice President supplier. My head was banging, buzzing and zonking. I thought I was coming down with death. I didn't understand what could make these weird feelings and sounds, where they were coming from and why. Somehow I got through it. My friend seemed anxious to get me a drink, a diet coke, as we sat together before going into the meeting room at a local hotel. I slowly realized what had happened – I helped him paint his house and in the process, I avoided alcoholic beverages when we were painting. He knew I was a target. He had the diet coke in his hand. The next day I confronted him and said, "I thought you were my friend."

Less than a year later after leaving St. Louis, I accepted a job with a division of United Technologies. The "mickey" pusher had the nerve to call me and ask for a job. He had been fired. My eyes narrowed – I had already fired him as a friend. Sorry, no job.

Now in Detroit as a Director of Marketing in a division of United Technologies with responsibility for product management, advertising, and ten professionals plus about thirty-five national sales representatives of high technology products, my salary increased significantly from my days at BF Goodrich. At Goodrich my salary had increased eighteen percent over the three years I was there, from 1969 to 1972. Since leaving there my salary had increased two hundred and thirty-one percent over the last three years from 1972 to 1975. Had I remained in the same position at BF Goodrich, I would have been way behind and attained an annual salary increase at a maximum of five to ten percent for the three year period, in total.

I felt I was now at par with my former 1958 classmates, who had graduated on time from the University of Akron in 1962, perhaps even more than par. Since beginning work in 1967, with Goodyear Aerospace my salary had increased 375%. But, Akron University isn't a Harvard University, by a long shot.

Detroit lasted for three years and while I wasn't done yet, I felt a need to find a company and a city where we could sink our roots. We always sought a position in Akron and wanted to get back into the Akron area, but never made it. Part of the reason why is centered on Akron's large rubber companies – they were on their way down and out. Other associated and ancillary companies floundered. Over the next several years while still in Detroit, the Akron economy faltered. General Tire closed down, Firestone was sold to Bridgestone, BF Goodrich and its headquarters where I worked was sold to Uniroyal, and the headquarters building sold. Akron's tire production all but ceased. Akron, the rubber capital of the world was now left to Goodyear. Thereafter, a large exodus of white collar high paying jobs left Akron, Ohio.

What would be next? Same song, same verse, a little bit better, a little bit worse.

1977 to 1988

During late summer and fall of 1976, my dad's verbal and mental faculties declined due to his illness from glioblastoma progression. Around Thanksgiving he had been given a go-ahead to be transferred from home to a sanatorium in Springfield Township. The facility located at the top of a hill in Lakemore overlooking Sanatorium Road was the same place Grandpa Henry had been taken to convalesce from a stroke a number of years earlier when he lived in Akron.

After a 1975 diagnosis, surgery, and chemotherapy Dad lived another eighteen months. We were only four hours away in Milford, Michigan, and were able to travel to Akron many times following his surgery and recuperation. Mom had been his primary caretaker and emotional support, along with my sister Nancy's good help and my brother's companionship during this time. He fought against cancer doing everything the doctor's asked of him, but he passed away at fifty-eight years on February 10, 1977, on my brother's thirty-eighth birthday.

It was a life totally spent on his family – working and taking chances to increase his income and building a better life for his family than either he or Mom had when they were young. He lived a life without flinching. Dad was well loved.

We walked together and talked about many things, but it wasn't enough. I still miss him.

At my desk in Detroit in the spring of 1977, I opened the Wall Street Journal Employment Section. An ad caught my eye. The advertisement was for a Director of Industrial Marketing for a newly formed capital equipment division. Interested replies were directed to send a resume to a post office box number. I threw my hat into the ring. In a couple of weeks my phone rang and it was the company's Director of Human Resources calling to set up a preliminary phone interview.

A few weeks after the phone interview, I met the Vice President and President of the company and found out the company was located in Middletown, Ohio. They emphasized the over fifty-year-old company operated as a family unit, looking out for each other. The president fostered the philosophy of paternalism and believed it created an atmosphere of good will. I would be reporting to the Vice President of Marketing. They stated I was "their kind of people," and I would "wear well" over the long haul. Both held high level positions at National Cash Register in Dayton. They set up a tour of their manufacturing facility and office, with an invitation for both my wife and me to visit Middletown within the next few weeks. I was impressed with them and their professional approach in the discussions. That was a good start.

We moved into Middletown at the end of June, 1977, about three hours' driving time from Akron. I was ready to apply the brakes on job-hopping in return for a stable company and job situation. Our youngsters were becoming young men, our daughter was entering her teen years and our youngest son was entering the third grade. Changing schools on-average every two years was getting harder and harder with each of them having to leave friends and start all over developing their standing in a new school environment. There was more resistance to change. We had to settle down, if possible.

After one year in the new job in the new city of Middletown, Ohio, we invested a portion of our savings into a retail business that we initiated from scratch located at a newly built mall, the Towne Mall in Middletown. This would be our first attempt at going into business on our own without any prior kind of experience. We hesitated getting into a franchise situation due to the belief we would not be in charge of our fortunes. We didn't want someone looking over our shoulders and being responsible to them for franchise and other fees amounting to thousands of dollars that would otherwise be left in our pockets and to our discretion. I would continue working at my job while Marilyn would run the retail operation. It wasn't a big time deal, just a pipe, tobacco, and gift shop. However, it was a big deal in that we had no experience in retail store ownership, nor in the pipe and tobacco business. This was a big step with commitments.

Vicki in Marilyn's
old costume

I smoked a pipe for several years off and on. That was it. That was the sum total of our experience level. In order to compensate for our lack of experience and knowledge, I visited a number of pipe shops located in malls covertly stepping off distances from this counter to that counter, this display to that one, and mentally calculating space requirements for a walk-in humidor. It was an important part of the planning process because we were limited to a 1,000 square foot space that was unimproved with a dirt gravel floor base and no walls. It was literally a rectangular box with nothing there. All of the mechanicals, plumbing, and electrical had to be built from the ground floor up. I had to evaluate the space with flashlight in hand since no lights existed in the space. Construction contracts had to be signed and attorneys involved.

We gained further understanding by flying into New York City in the summer of 1978, to attend an annual pipe, cigar, and tobacco trade show. This trip allowed us to visit with all of the necessary vendors including pocket lighter and gift manufacturers who were all present in one place, The Waldorf Astoria, where we stayed for a couple of days.

Marilyn was a great partner in this crazy thing we had gotten ourselves into and she did it with full understanding and control of mind and body in the whole undertaking. Where did we get all of this "chutzpah?" I don't know. We decided we were going to do it and we did it. We opened the doors in November, 1978. It worked!

Covertly, we were becoming concerned about the company I had joined. Cracks began to appear as travel budgets were reduced and some people were told their jobs were going to be absorbed. A quiet and disquieting atmosphere dominated the office during the start of the second half of 1978. In essence we looked upon the investment into the retail business as a pseudo protective device, not enough to bank on, but a stab at getting our feet wet in a business that we, at least, controlled. It helped us believe we could make it work and possibly settle down.

I bet you guessed right. A year later in August, 1979, I was advised my job would be phased into another department with a lower level office manager handling the salesmen I'd hired and running the structure I'd developed over the last two years. The manager, who was in his late fifties seemed pained when I turned over my company car keys and showed him the records and people he'd need to manage. When I told him I'd planted fruit trees at home representing our decision to settle down in Middletown, he winced and shook his head. They downsized me.

Before I lost my job in August, I personally witnessed a terrible accident – a young man's life stopped in Boston, Massachusetts, on Boylston Street at an intersection in early March at about eight-thirty in the evening. It was dark, but street lights were bright. After completing the second day of a trade show, I took a walk to finish off the evening. I stopped at a traffic light. The young man wore a baseball cap, and was riding a skinny-tire Schwinn bicycle peddling fast through the intersection under a green light when a twenty-foot white box truck turned left and plowed into him with the grill of the truck. His thin body immediately whipped under the truck, smashing his head on the pavement and was pinned down, getting tangled in the crumpled and tumbling bicycle. The driver sitting high didn't see him over the hood, or he may have been completely distracted by something and kept driving at moderate speed not knowing a bicyclist was under his truck mortally injured. If the force of his head hitting the street didn't kill him, surely the dragging and crumpling intertwined together with the bicycle would have, as his body skidded along the pavement.

People on the sidewalk waved their hands and yelled at the driver to stop, trying to get his attention. He had no idea why they were waving and shouting in his direction, but about a block from the impact, he stopped in the middle of the four lane two-way street. When I caught up with the truck I could see dark shiny liquid pooling around the cyclist's body and head. His time stopped for good. He had no idea as he rode his bike under the green light it would be for the last time. Others gathered around in the middle of the street. Cars stopped. I kept walking with regret – I had no way to prevent or help him avoid the collision. It happened so fast, nobody could have helped him. Sirens wailed in the distance. That night I thought about how short and unfair life can be.

What was I going to do, now? Every move I made problems followed, it seemed.

I sent out resumes and contacted headhunters in Dayton, Cincinnati, and beyond. It was an old familiar thing by now. In the last twelve years which didn't seem long, I had worked at a number of companies for about the same number of reasons. So it wasn't a new experience. As a matter of fact, I was predicting outcomes before I walked into any interview based on telephone interviews and my predilection of company size and culture. Many companies were starting up new product opportunities just like the company in Middletown, a new industrial division based on some new whiz-bang product that would need a new leader with experience.

That was me.

The problem was these companies if not on a stock exchange, they held the company's profit and loss statements close to their chests and didn't divulge information. If owned by a holding company it was even more difficult, like my latest employer. And that was key to many problems in the late sixties and seventies. Takeovers and wholesale diversity of product impelled companies to do all kind of tricks to show better annual results. In the process a lot of people got trampled.

That, too, was me.

The old standby, paternalism in business was gone. A new norm developed – making orphans without remorse. The management did what had to be done, or were told to do, in order to keep companies viable and to save the jobs of those left behind, including the bosses.

My family and I, all six of us, were without an income, with nowhere to go to replace our livelihood. Unemployment was available, but it was second, third choice, or last choice as far as I was concerned. A job was needed.

Fortunately, my resumes were effective. I had several interviews. Even though short stints were obvious, job-hopping was now viewed as a faster way to gain experience. If someone showed enhanced responsibility coupled with salaried growth, that person was deemed more valuable for the task they had open, or had created.

We were all getting tired of moving. The thought of pulling up stakes again wasn't appealing at all. It was minor, but every time we moved, I think something got lost.

On one of my interviews in early November, I put my suitcase together for a trip to an interview in the Pittsburgh area. I realized my light trench coat was missing. We couldn't find it anywhere. I had to leave. I ran out to Penny's on the way to the airport and bought a tan trench coat for the trip. It came in handy as the temperature dropped in Pittsburgh that night. In the morning I went through the motions of another interview process. On the way back from lunch with three people from the office, I was aware that the two walking behind the boss and me were kind of snickering. What was that about? I wondered.

Mom, Nancy and Patty

Boarding the flight back, I stuffed the trench coat in the overhead bin above my seat. During the rough flight the bin must have jarred loose after not being closed securely, and a tan coat sleeve dangled down from the bin. I looked up and out of the sleeve popped a price tag attached to a three inch nylon fastening string. The price, $149.99 in bold type. It was my coat. I hadn't removed the tag! I'd gone to lunch with a potential boss with a price tag hanging down from the new tan trench coat.

What embarrassment must I have caused the people meeting me for the first time? I'm sure the snickering concerned the hanging price tag and a well-placed comment about Minnie Pearl of Grand Old Opry fame and the price tag on her bonnet. She used the tag as a joke. I was the joke. I didn't get a chance to play along with this one as I did with Joe McMullen's castigating act during football practice at Akron's Buchtel Field twenty years ago in 1959.

I was beginning to lose enthusiasm for and getting tired of the interviewing process as the weeks moved along. I began to look at the possibility of expanding our foray into retail mall operations. The appeal of running our business full time appeared to satisfy our recent need to settle down and get off of the new job, new city, new school, new everything merry-go-round.

Marilyn was supportive of making the transition to one hundred percent self-employment, so that's what we did. I began scouting for a new mall location that may provide an opportunity for higher profit potential than did our location at Towne Mall in Middletown. The only nearby mall absent a pipe and tobacco gift shop was located in Springfield, Ohio, at the Upper Valley Mall. There were two competitors within a twenty minute drive from this location, one of which was well known, but both were definitely marketing challenges. It was either the Springfield location or none.

My oldest son, Rick, and I began the construction task of converting an existing space into our design in June, 1980. It was about the same size and shape of our Middletown operation. After four weeks of long hours and sore muscles and an hour's drive from home, we opened the store at the Upper Valley Mall in July, 1980. We had reduced the cost significantly by doing the work ourselves and with only a neon sign sub-contractor the job was completed. It conformed to our original design in Middletown and looked like a well-known brand, The Tinder Box.

The Springfield location's performance went way beyond expectations in its first year's volume and profitability levels. The actual results were two hundred and ninety percent above our original store's results – that's three times better.

Big Bad Bill's Soap Box Derby

Over the next six years we opened an athletic footwear shop and three more pipe and tobacco shops. Not all were as successful as Springfield, but it was a success in providing self-employment for myself and family. But all was not well when at one mall location the mall management permitted a major competitor in athletic footwear to open a new store in 1983. There were too many competitors in the local foot wear market.

I filed legal action against the mall management company on the basis of constructive eviction – we lost. We were going to be in for a rough time.

It was a very rough time. We had to bite the bullet. By January, 1987, we had divested ourselves of the athletic footwear shop and three pipe and tobacco gift shop locations. Finally, we retained only one shop and had sold the rest including Springfield as market conditions turned unfavorable. The idea of being self-employed lasted for ten years. What to do now? It didn't take long to go back to the drawing board consider the overall situation and come up with a new plan.

The new plan wasn't very new. I spent time in early 1987, sending out resumes. In April, a company in North Carolina responded via a head hunter with an offer to travel to Charlotte for a required comprehensive interview to include a psychological profile and intelligence testing.

Testing wasn't a new thing. The steel company in St. Louis required the same kind of testing for its job. Others required the same thing during interviews. I wasn't disturbed by it, although it can be exhausting if you really need a job and if they "grill" you extensively. I completed the testing at the head hunter's offices. I flew home and waited to see if I passed satisfactorily enough to receive the company's name, location, and date for an in-depth personal interview with the hiring authority. Word came back, an interview was scheduled for late June – the company was located in Charlotte, North Carolina; Pneumafil Corporation. It was a division of a Swiss company at the time. They designed and built high quality rugged metal enclosures for military, aerospace, and commercial markets, plus computer cabinets primarily for Aegis class cruisers and destroyers for the Navy. They also manufactured products for industrial dust collection.

Marilyn and I had to prepare for the possibility of moving to Charlotte. Marilyn was working at Paper Systems

Incorporated in Miamisburg, Ohio, a little south of Dayton. Her mother, Bea, moved to Middletown in February, 1986, to be near us after her husband and Marilyn's father, Bill, had died in 1985. Our youngest son, Bill, had one more semester of high school to complete by the end of 1987. So there were several pieces of interconnected parts to consider in making a move to Charlotte if things materialized.

I needed to find a job and was looking forward to securing a good paying position in spite of the complicated logistics of keeping things together, family-wise, including Marilyn's mother.

June's interview went well. But I was left a little less than enthusiastic when the general manager who I'd report to said,

"Some people say I'm hard to work for." Then he asked, "What do you think about that?"

I looked him in the eyes and said, "Not much." I paused, "If I do the job that needs done, I don't see any problem."

He smiled.

It took several more weeks, but I finally got the call by the middle of August 1987. I was offered the job as the company marketing manager responsible for a division and a machine shop company they purchased several years prior; combined they had a low eight figure annual revenue. It was not what I really wanted to hear. They were looking for product development and other metal fabrication opportunities. They were large enough to offer direct payment for the move from Middletown, Ohio, to Charlotte, N.C., plus lodging expenses during the move for Bea and ourselves. If not, we wouldn't have gone. I accepted the offer with a starting date of October 26, 1987. This date seemed prescient, later, after all of the changes we experienced as the weeks following my acceptance fell into place.

The news from Akron in October was a terrible shock. My mother died of heart failure from congestive heart disease. She was living with my sister, Nancy, and had not given any indication of being in any immediate trouble. As she lived she had died, ready to help anyone and without on ounce of complaint she passed on. A few years earlier she told me about a dream she had about my father who'd passed away in 1977. In the dream she walked up several floors as she got to the top floor, Dad told her "It's not time yet. You have to go back." The last time I visited her in Akron was near her birthday on March 21, 1987, six months earlier on my way home from Cleveland. When I was about to leave I hugged her, and said, "You've been a good Mom." She beamed. I wish I'd said, "A great mom," because she was. My mom didn't drink. She smoked cigarettes while suffering emphysema, but she finally stopped the habit in 1983. She enjoyed the last years of her life driving to visit her sisters and her brother in Niles. Things changed, though, as events caused her driving license to be taken away during her last year.

Her condition began a slow, but recognizable decline when she lost consciousness and fell to the floor while standing in line at a funeral, two days before Mother's Day in 1986. She ended up in a hospital in Ravenna, Ohio, where the funeral had taken place. She was under heavy sedation when my wife and I visited her. She was diagnosed with hypoxia, a lack of oxygen supplying her organs and she also had pneumonia. She talked with us, but she was in and out of consciousness. We stayed for a while as the attendants came to thump her back to break up the secretions in her lungs. It was sad to watch. Her body was losing weight and it was difficult for her to move. They told us she would be okay soon, so we left and headed back home to Middletown. The next day my brother called from the hospital. He said Mom didn't remember we had been there to see her. I called and commiserated with her about her condition.

A year later in late May 1987, we received a call from my brother that she was in an accident and again in the hospital. She was driving and at fault, but he said it wasn't bad. She had bruises, but nothing serious and would be out in another day. The medics took her to the hospital to be safe. I only talked with her by phone. When I stopped by my sister's house in March on my way home from Cleveland, it would be the last time I saw her.

Daisy, Mom, Esther,   *and Uncle Kenny*

No one can ever repay a good mother for what they've done, not on this earth, nor in heaven. It's a magical thing mothers do for their children from the time of conception to death. They are forever bound to their children come pestilence or plague, they will hug you forever.

I miss my mom and think of her often.

So it was. On Monday, October 12, 1987, my mother, Eva, suddenly passed away. I didn't know her time was that short. I believed she would continue to press on as she had done for the last ten years or more. She was always ready for a smile and laugh. She had a delightfully hearty laugh you could count on to envelope your thoughts and make you feel better even if you didn't want to feel better. It was a sad day for all of us, her extended family and friends.

Seven days later, the stock market suffered its largest loss in its history - $500 billion in one day was wiped out. Seven days later after the market decline, I began working in Charlotte. Was it auspicious or a precursor of bad news to come?

I felt bad and down, going to Charlotte only 14 days after Mom had died and then Black Monday occurring on October 19, 1987, the day that marked the beginning of a global market decline. I had to shake it off after signing on and living out of a hotel to start the new job on October 26. I needed to find a home to accommodate all four of us, Bea, Bill, Marilyn and myself. At work the first hint of "bad news to come" was upon learning a consultant group had been hired in mid-November "to help get us on track, financially." By that point in time, a newly built house was under contract in Matthews, North Carolina. A scheduled move-in date was December 18, 1987, one week before Christmas.

I packed my bags, took a few days off from work and headed home to see if I could do anything to help get things in order for the moving company. They were ready to pick up Marilyn's mom's belongings, our household goods, and to transport them to our new home in Charlotte. The moving coordination and certain boxed items fell on Marilyn's shoulders again. With some trepidation concerning the "consultants," we stepped into the unknown opened up a little wider by the "Black Monday" historic market shock. Too soon in January, 1988, the unknown became known. I ran across an advertisement in the Wall Street Journal. A small ad for a Quality Control Manager. The ad style, size and wording was familiar. It was the same size and format as the ad for a Marketing Manager I responded to seven months earlier. The ad was most likely placed by the same head hunter. "Looks like they're going to replace the existing Q.C. Manager they had just hired before me," I thought. I didn't say anything to anyone.

My tenure was only three months old, or less, if you subtract the holidays – make it two and one-half months total. I began looking over my shoulder to see who was sneaking up on me. Could they be thinking about replacing me after just moving into a new house, with our existing house in Middletown up for sale and my mother-in-law and our youngest son, Bill, who would join us shortly? Is that what they were up to?

Well it didn't seem so. My interactions with my boss were all good. He congratulated me on a company meeting that I initiated for developing strategy and advertising programs. I prepared a five-year business plan for existing military products and was in the process of developing a territorial sales strategy to bring sales reps inside, rather than being remotely positioned in the existing structure. During this time I heard nothing about the consultants. But interestingly, Charley, the sales manager stepped into my office. He had a big grin on his face and began a one-way dialogue about a funny story that made him laugh, not me – the story had no bearing on anything. All he wanted to do was smile and laugh.

Maybe he (Charlie) was going to be my Tommy Evans, the backfield coach at The University of Akron who separated me from my quarterback position.

My boss wanted me to know early on that Charley, the sales manager, was going to be replaced. I never considered he was going to be a problem. The only other possible thing I could think of was that I had been asked during the initial interviews if I smoked cigarettes. Apparently the general manager of the machine shop was allergic to cigarette smoke, because I think he was a converted cigarette smoker himself. When asked I said,

"No," because I had never smoked cigarettes. No one asked if I smoked a pipe. I didn't say I smoked a pipe.

At the end of January, management called a meeting of the company personnel. We were informed the consultants finished their work. The conclusion of their investigation was that management would have to reduce head count by 20%. "Look around," the general manager said, "One in five of you will have to find another job soon. We'll let you know who as soon as possible." On February 21, 1988, he let me know. He said I could use my office and desk, and use any of the office services to find another position for as long as necessary, but my salary would end in thirty days.

Was it Charley the sales manager? Was it because I smoked a pipe occasionally at lunch? Was it my pipe? The President of the company smoked a pipe. When I interviewed with him he smoked his pipe. I didn't. We talked about pipe tobacco and about various well known pipe brands. We had good rapport as a result. No, it wasn't my pipe; no it wasn't Charlie. I think Charlie was happy because he'd gotten a heads-up from someone who knew the result of the consultants' summary, and he would most likely be saying "goodbye" to me. No, it wasn't anything anyone had done, it was the historic market loss and the "small company syndrome," i.e., it was a small company getting too big for its britches. The division should have stayed the way it had been. They didn't need a marketing manager.

After the general manager had given me the news and offered to let me use the services of the office, he asked if I wanted to know why I was on the list. I said, "No." He looked surprised. I didn't want to give him any reason to make up excuses. I'm sure he had one prepared, but I didn't want any of it. It was my only offensive move and I wasn't going to lose it. For the next three months from March to May I went to my office and contacted as many companies as I could where I thought there may be a fit. Rubbermaid, STP, a local steel distributor, and others were visited in person, but the story was the same, "When the economy improves, we'll want to talk with you further." Marilyn and I couldn't be waiting around for that to happen. She had obtained a temporary position with an accounting firm in the area. It helped with the expenses. Bill got a job at a Tinder Box smoke shop in a mall close by in the Charlotte area.

My boss, mentioned if I needed help to let him know. I did. We sat down. I advised him of my results in the local market and told him what I'd really like is to be able to move back to Middletown. Our house hadn't sold as yet. I asked him if it was possible for the company to pay for a return move of our household goods including two stops – one at our house and one at an apartment nearby for my mother-in-law including an automobile to transport.

He said, "Let me see if I can get that done."

Fortunately, the answer was, "Yes."

On May 26, 1988, exactly seven months from the day I began the Pneumafil caper, the movers came to our house in Matthews, N.C. and rescued my wife, my mother-in-law, my son, and me, and moved all of our belongings back to Middletown – where they belonged. My tail was between my legs. We had to face our family, our neighbors, and look for employment.

We stuck a "For Sale" sign in the yard and left Charlotte, North Carolina.

1988 to 2022

Our house was still there when Marilyn and I arrived in Middletown. We opened the front door. The house had the feel of an unoccupied empty house, but our emotions didn't feel any hurt or have a trace of sadness. To the contrary, we were full of gratitude that we could return to our home and leave the Charlotte experience behind.

The house had been freshly painted when we left, in a "ready to sell" condition five months earlier. It still had the fresh paint new house smell permeating the air inside. We smiled at each other with a measure of satisfaction that we were once again moving into the house on Carlow Circle, the house and the neighborhood we had chosen in 1977, for our family. We spent ten years living there during the time our kids were growing up.

The moving boxes were placed in each room as marked by the moving company. It didn't take us long to get all of the furniture moved into place, organized, and all other items in place that are associated with a full house move. We weren't new to the routine after having moved from New York City in

1964 to Akron, and then, west to St. Louis in 1974 with a number of other moves and stops in between over the last twenty-four years. Fortunately, we didn't have to bear any of the costs associated with moving our family during those years.

We didn't have anything to learn about Middletown. It was the easiest move we had ever made to any new house in any part of the country. We were settled in from the very first day in the house. Marilyn had obtained employment two years ago in 1986, for a paper converting company with slitting and printing capability for paper rolls and fax paper. In a week or two after we returned, she contacted the owner of the company. They welcomed her with open arms and she began working there again. She would do extremely well and go on to become their office manager with marketing responsibility. All things considered, it was time for me to find another position – a job.

It didn't take long before Marilyn heard me say, "Let's send out some resumes."

Marilyn at Paper Systems Inc.

"Oh no. Not that again," we both thought. Another upset another potential move. I wasn't getting any younger, now approaching forty nine years of age with a wild and wooly industrial and self-employed retail background. Who would take the chance? Let's find out.

It took nearly six months before I reported for duty in Cincinnati during February, 1989, as head of a new product opportunity. "Not again, not another new product." This employer was headquartered in Cincinnati, a manufacturer of industrial products and commercial pollution control equipment, with international sales and production facilities located in England and Japan. I reported to the President of the company; he and the Chairman of the Board were great people and I immediately felt comfortable with both of them. They allowed me to set goals, develop a plan, and hire competent people to interface with a customer base that had to be established from the ground floor to whatever level we achieved.

Things couldn't have gone better. Sales and engineering had to work closely together. I hired new people to serve different end users than with the company's original products. Over a seven year period our sales of the new product marketed primarily to steel and food producers increased from trial equipment initially to millions of dollars. We outsold and out marketed existing competitors including the major market supplier.

At one point I thought it might be a good time to find out if the major market supplier would have an interest in selling their company. Basically – we had overtaken them in the largest market segment, the steel producing market. Our success most likely damaged their profit/loss structure. I felt like a clairvoyant after talking with our president. We approached them through a third party and found out they were in fact seeking a buyer. We made an offer, but employees ended up buying the company. The writing was on the wall.

Things change. I was promoted to Vice President and given more product responsibility about two years before an authentic sell-takeover rumor of our own company surfaced. I didn't want to wait around for the internal fights for power to begin. The outcome, problems, and concerns about a takeover had already reared its ugly face. My age was a deficit. I was now in my mid-fifties. I knew it would be a fight not easily won and based on current happenings, I could be left in the cold, "on the outside, looking in." I had to make a decision – to wait it out or resign.

I decided to resign. It was 1995. Without any fanfare I talked with head hunters and briefly considered some employment opportunities, but how many times would I have to return to this watering hole with the time I had left prior to retirement?

"What to do? What to do?"

Why not try something different, for a change? What? What did I say? That's all I've been doing my whole life. So why change now, something different always appealed to me. I sat down at my desk opened the phone book and became a personnel recruiter, a "head hunter" as the identification of the position is and always will be, most likely. I was not a head counter, a plant counter, a job hopper, or a job wanderer – I was a head hunter. Prior to embarking on such a polar career move, I investigated the job requirements when I talked with recruiters about possible employment. I learned the basics of how to get job orders, to specialize or not, and a lot about setting up necessary government reporting records and other information. The other information included a "fly by the seat of your pants" ability to get the job accomplished.

I turned things around and upside down. Instead of being the hunted, I was now the hunter.

Is this for real? In my first twelve months I placed twenty-two people and had attained my highest ever income level. I had expenses but not that much with most cost going to recruiters with whom I shared fifty percent on split fees, taking my income after costs and expenses several levels into six figures. That's not nearly as much as a large corporation Vice President makes, but all things are relative. In my new position, I worked in my home office, took time off as I pleased, and conducted my business as I pleased. And, I didn't have a boss. I was very pleased. However, I worked hard, was disciplined and didn't take advantage of the newest success as I probably could have. Marilyn continued working and I was able to employ my sons in the business for a time when they thought it would be a good move for themselves to "learn the ropes."

I made calls to hiring managers at six-thirty to seven a.m. when I knew from talking with them it might be a time when they'd be in the office like, "What time do you get in the office?" an off-the-cuff question. They weren't upset I'd called. Conversely, I had more than one say they were impressed by my phone call so early – I took it as a positive. It was something that never happened with a recruiter before. Being an "early bird" had monetary rewards. As Benjamin Franklin would say in Poor Richard's Almanac, "Early to bed and early to rise makes a man healthy, wealthy, and wise."

My company offered a grocery tactic, "Buy five get one free." Five placements at one company was rewarded with the sixth placement free. No time restrictions, the sale was good for the foreseeable future. It worked. Over the course of one year, the tactic returned over $125,000 in real money from one company. There was no advertising about it, no hoopla, just a casual mention made hiring managers and human resources interested in doing business with me.

A paper equipment company gave me a job order for a General Manager with a starting salary at $100,000 plus incentives. It was at a 30% fee level. After about ten candidates had been interviewed over a four month period they called me in to meet with the Vice President and HR Manager. I was puzzled at first. The Vice President did all the talking indicating they had decided to pull the job order and would later determine if they wanted to continue the search. It was a disappointment to say the least.

"What we've decided to do is to give you $12,000 for the work you've done. Then we're going to review this to determine what we'll do," he said. "That's a surprise and a great offer, but I can't accept. I didn't do the job," I quickly replied, without even giving it a thought. It just wasn't right for them to pay me for non-performance. It was very generous of them but it just didn't feel right.

They both looked at each other. The HR Manager spoke up.

"We want you to have this, Don," the HR Manager said.

"Thank you, very much, but I can't accept it," I said.

 Again, they both looked at each other.

"Okay then, we'll get back in touch with you," the Vice President said. I was baffled on the way home. Why did they want to do that? I had a very good relationship with them, but the $12,000 was a free gift.

A week later, the HR Manager called.

"Don, we've been talking with a candidate for the General Manager's position. We want you to meet with him and give us your impressions of his fit for the position. We think he's the right guy for the job, but we'd like you to talk with him."

"Sure, I'd like to do that."

"He's going to call you. If we hire Bill we'll pay you the fee involved," he said.

I got the call from Bill and we met at a Bob Evans' Restaurant at the Dayton Mall. It turned out he was an individual who had been told earlier that I was looking for a General

Manager. In my job search a friend of Bill's who worked with him, told me to call Bill. I had called Bill, but he never called back and I had never been able get in touch with him. It isn't unusual people don't call head hunters back, if they aren't interested in a job change.

Bill apparently contacted the company on his own without calling me, thinking he'd save the prospective company a recruiting fee. That must have been how the offer of $12,000 came about and why I was seated at a breakfast table with Bill. This was a rubber stamp deal. He was subsequently hired and the company honored my work with a check for $30,000. If I would have accepted the offer of $12,000, I probably would have never known it was Bill who had been hired due to my effort. The company gained my respect and I gained their trust in an altogether innocent way.

During the last years of my working life as a head hunter, I placed many people in engineering, sales, production, personnel, purchasing, and management positions from 1995 to 2002. My hope is that the people I placed have been able to overcome all of the challenges a working life presents. From the way things look it isn't going to get any easier and the opportunities for growth and change will be ever present in the careers they choose.

Working allowed us to build a new home in a golf course community near Middletown, Ohio, in Springboro. I retired early at sixty-two and Marilyn retired later at sixty-seven years of age. We were both free from a regular schedule and pursued our own interests and whatever we decided to do at the time.

I started up an old pursuit and made paintings in acrylic and oils eventually painting enough canvases to have my daughter, Vicki, develop a web site and join Fine Art America. com, a print to order company. I also completed an initial genealogy for the Henrys and Marilyn's family, the Mellers. Marilyn has been able to spend more time reading and visiting with friends and family. Our son, Rick, has two daughters, Doug also has two daughters, Vicki has two daughters and a son, and Bill has one son. We also have three great granddaughters at this point. It's hard to believe that Rick and Doug are in their sixties and Vicki and Bill are in their fifties. We're much too young to have children that old aren't we?

Vicki's Wedding
Doug, Vicki, Rick, and Bill

In my experience over the last 50 years or more, it's difficult for me to determine which choice I prefer, "Soft" Paternalism or Self-Determination. I believe an individual has to be prepared to make a difficult choice and make a success of it, and always be ready to make needed changes. Regardless of which is chosen, either one is a gamble, because of vicissitudes – the unknowable conditions and changes in the market place, including the forces of competition and economic dynamics. For instance, who would have guessed the internet would take over and dominate consumer shopping as has happened. Who would have guessed there would be an internet? The large indoor malls had a lock on the market and put smaller strip centers and mom and pop shops out of business. Now malls are vacant, closed and are closing up. This is happening due to the speed with which change is occurring.

At some point self-determination such as investing your money, your time and your future into a business to offset the everyday worry and hunt for a better job will be attractive. But you have to be careful, the golden ring you strain to reach might turn out to be a rusty carbon steel ring that has several layers of gold spray paint. It happens. It happened to my dad, and it happened to me as a job-hopper and as a self-determination participant.

And, there is a caveat – you won't go wrong if you add a hefty amount of perseverance in your approach to anything that prevents you from achieving success – but, it may take a while.

It's been an interesting, frustrating, disappointing, rewarding, lucky, and happy trip at times. Once around is enough, I think, unless life-hopping becomes discovered in some new electronic or cryogenic product development laboratory, unlike the nightmarish dreams of the Frankenstein character I had had on Talbot Avenue.

My early life and background with my mom and dad contributed to the learnings and lessons gleaned from a life filled with humps and bumps. I saw first-hand what positive things resulted for my dad from seeking new companies and employment when improvement in income was needed. I also found out what risks lie in wait for those who take it upon themselves to start up their own businesses when they are not satisfied working for someone else.

I developed a one track mind to do whatever is necessary to seek a higher income resulting in a better standard of living. I was bent on improvement and financial security as a goal, however spastic and crazy things had become at some points along the way. I didn't want to be on the poor side of the tracks, the tracks where many of our relatives found themselves, with no way to jump over and get out. I knew a college education was necessary. It was a way to fly over the constraints that forced people into jobs they were compelled to continue. With a college degree I believed my spirit could fly without constraint. The sky was limitless.

As things turned out, I approached everything in military fashion, "double-time x 2." I couldn't wait to get into grade school. Then I sat in school watching slow motion clocks burn time each day with days getting longer and longer; it would take forever to get on a faster time schedule. Then, I couldn't wait to get out of grade school. In high school time broke its chains and began to move a bit more in tune with what was happening. We had more freedom to choose the things we wanted to do. Once you get out of high school, graduate and move on to an occupation or college and then possibly get married, there is a rush of life that you become a part of, but you can't see it happening. When you were in grade school, things happened slowly and you had no cares in the world other than your next birthday party or what you might get for Christmas or Easter. Then, much later time flies. You begin to concern yourself with things like how your family or kids are doing. Are they healthy with enough internal strength to come out on top of disappointments and medical issues they may encounter?

When you stop to review the reasons for past events they become less fuzzy and have more clarity. It's like looking through the wrong end of binoculars or a telescope, everything's in view, but much farther away. Whether the review creates feelings of regret, resentment or pride, you realize that no one makes the best choice in every situation. It helps to understand the how and why "those" things occurred. It's your history. No one else can make a claim as to how they may have reacted. It's yours alone to celebrate or mourn. It's part of who you are. It's how it developed your outlook and made you a better person, because you were there.

We are all connected in some way. How we are connected is up to us to find out.

One of the more interesting and relevant aspects to come out of my search was a fact my first cousin, Matt Dexter, a top notch genealogy and DNA researcher, advised me about. It concerned my Grandma Henry. I don't think anyone in the Henry family knew about this, or has known this. Legally she was a Norris; DNA-wise no she wasn't, and therefore, I am not a Norris either. The reason I'm bummed about it is because, the earliest ancestor I've listed on the Henry-Norris genealogy chart is Thomas Edward Norris, Sr., born in 1608 in Norfolk, England, who ran away from home when he was eleven years old. He didn't run away to join the circus, but to become a cabin boy on an ocean-going vessel.

No, Thomas isn't the Jim Hawkins of "Treasure Island." This boy is a real life person. As a result of his gumption and subsequent sailor's life, in 1630, he landed in Nansemond County, Virginia, and remained in America until his death. He was the first person with the surname, Norris, to be recorded in this part of Colonial America. He became an entrepreneur, a trader, a landowner, and a planter who owned and sold land in the tobacco heartland and traveled in better societal circles. A book was written about him titled, "Thomas Norris – The Immigrant," by Pearl Mitchell Mallory. He was a go-getter, someone like him I had hoped to find in our bloodline. What a surprise to find a kindred spirit, who had done the kind of things I had done: starting disparate businesses not knowing how they would turn out but always open to new product opportunities. I sighed. Well, maybe Norris genes would be weaker, anyway, having traveled down the ancestry chart a ways. Maybe now you can understand why I'm disappointed to find Norris blood is not flowing, however slowly in my veins. I hoped and would like to have thought that's where my restless gumption and motivation comes from. Not so, it comes from my mom and dad. They had persevered and diligently worked through their misfortunes.

It turns out John David Norris, the second Great Grandfather on my Grandma Henry's side was not sired by John

Wesley Norris. John David Norris's father was Thomas Atwell, who had died early when John David was only four year's old. Then his mother, Margaret Polly Songer, married John Wesley Norris. When I found out about this news, from Matt Dexter, my cousin on my father's side, I traced Thomas Atwell back to 1530 in England to Thomas Attawell. Yes, the name had changed to Atwell going forward. No kings or queens were found in the castles of England.

So, I have to accept my Grandma Henry wasn't a Norris and my genes changed overnight, form Norris to Atwell. Again, I lost some enthusiasm about my Henry history, but interestingly, one of the first and only visitor we had in Sandusky, Ohio, from the commanding Salvation Army Headquarters in Cleveland was a Major Atwell, who was in charge of Finance. "Hmmm. Makes you think, doesn't it. We are all connected, aren't we?

I decided to keep the genealogy chart as is, with regard to the adoption. It's perfectly legal as is, from John David on down to Margaret Ann Henry (Norris). Of course, I didn't know all of this in 1968. I would have studied Major Atwell more carefully, listened to him more intently, while carefully remembering his facial features, and characteristics as if I had already known him for a long time, from long ago.

Our Heatherwoode House

Whatever happens in your life you realize – it's the life you own. Things happen from time to time, but you have the steering wheel in your hands. You guide your own trip down life's road and make decisions you think are best at the time. Sometimes it's good, sometimes not, but you can't go back and change things. My decisions are over. I don't believe there are any major decisions left to fret over. In a way it's a sad thing to say and to realize. In another way I sigh and think to myself, "That's a relief." My hands are calm and relaxed as I loosen my grip on the steering wheel. Important decisions are in the rear-view mirror. The colors and textures of my life have been established.

If I didn't agree with management, needed to increase my salary, or if I was getting bored I looked for another job inside or outside the company. If that's not a good thing in your mind, consider this – sometimes leaving is more difficult than staying. Staying, in essence, might become the easy way out. But, I think it's the least good choice. It slowly changes your spirit. You give up.

When you leave things that are known and safe, you have everything to lose. Some say you should stay and work it out, that's the honorable thing to do. Yes, it may be honorable, but it gives you **no** opportunity to find the things you are seeking, whether that be a better job, a higher standard of living, a new life, a thirst for knowledge, a chance to utilize all of your abilities in an effort to accomplish goals, a healthier less-stressed life, or any of the positive things associated with a life that has been well-lived. Companies don't hesitate to put together a list of people to fire or lay off when they send jobs to foreign countries or need to increase profits. However, before you are hired, they pour over your background and have you take tests, see psychologists and set up several different people to grill you before they make a decision to hire you. When it comes time to reduce the ranks or reorganize, they smile and simply say, "Goodbye," if that. They do it because they can.

Is that honorable? They are the ones providing paychecks. They must make the difficult decisions. Maybe they should have not hired you, in the first place.

Would I have taken back anything in my life that I changed? Yes, with hind-sight. I would be hiding behind a lie if I said, "No, everything I did was right." At the time my choices were right and I couldn't see how they may be wrong. I overcame the problems my haste had presented or created – maybe it was because of perseverance that I had the problems in the first place. If it wasn't for perseverance, though, and becoming determined to finish college with a degree or two, I would have retired, unhappily, from Goodyear's R&D lab and lost a most challenging, if not a crazy life. I gripped the steering wheel and changed directions more than once. Sometimes I changed up things at the urging of an internal motivator or when "change was thrust upon me" and had I no choice, but to persevere. Perseverance is good.

Mothers and some fathers in the animal kingdom will fight to the death for their brood. In our own animal kingdom it happens. Why am I saying this? Because my mom and dad would have done the same thing to protect their children. I may not have written enough about my mother in the pages of this book. Some vignettes lost to time stand out, when I think about the time we spent together.

I always helped Mom if I could when I was home. She liked to tell a story about being sick in bed, how proud she was that I, at nine years of age, went to the basement on Talbot Avenue washed and wrung clothes, used clothes pins and hung up the clothes to dry. She worried about all the clothes piling up for days and couldn't get out of bed. She smiled large, so happy I had done the washing. To me it was needed, so I helped her when she wasn't able to do the work.

A story she'd recount involved house maintenance and her penchant for upkeep and cleaning. I came home around nine-thirty one hot, muggy summer night to find her hanging wall paper in our home on Swineheart Road. She struggled with keeping it straight, matching seams, and dripping adhesive on the dining room floor. After looking at the two sheets she had hung, I gave her a hand. I had never hung wall paper before and at fifteen years old, it wasn't on my list of things to do. A severe thunderstorm developed, but we continued to hang paper into the night while thunder and lightning crackled and exploded, until we finished about one-thirty in the morning. The work was done and it looked good. We cleaned up the mess and tools when it was over. Mom was pleased.

Another time at fifteen, we drove downtown to pay an overdue bill. We had to find an office in a ten story building in Akron. She found the city administration office and we sat down waiting to be called to the front desk. In a few minutes Mom began discussing details of the problem with a clerk.

There seemed to be some problem or misunderstanding. The clerk called a manager over and the two of them gave Mom the third degree. He was in his middle forties with graying hair, wearing a bow tie and had a sharp little nose. The manager began demeaning my mom, and said, "If you deadbeats would pay your bills, we wouldn't have this kind of trouble." I got up from my chair and went to the desk, pointed my finger at the manager, leaned over and stared as cold-hearted a stare as I could make and told him, "Mister, you don't talk to my mom like that. We're not deadbeats. Take it back." The manager began stuttering, stepped back and said, "Well okay. We can work this out." My mom smiled. I sat down. On the way home she said how proud she was. I was surprised myself.

My mother was a good mom. In fact, she was a great Mom.

My father was a good dad. In fact, he was a great Dad.

And, I have a wife by my side for nearly sixty-five years and more, always looking out for my best interests. Our lives have been full with anticipation. There is no doubt she deserves a better life, a less stressful life, but at least with me by her side she hasn't been bored. There always has been something to be happy about, or sad about. But nothing to make us drift off into complacency. We've traveled enough to know what traveling is, and we're not required to do it anymore.

I hope to keep it this way.

As I round third base and head for home, I believe I can beat the outfielder's throw. The Umpire is watching me run. I drop down into a running slide heading toward home plate some eighty years later. The ball whizzes by my shoulder – the catcher leaps over me, yellow dust cascades and bellows in the air over our scrambling bodies – and the ball careens off of his protective mask, out of reach.

The Umpire in a dark blue uniform straightens up his hunched-over back.

He remains silent, doesn't stick his thumb into the air.

Instead, he crosses his arms and waves me safe! He didn't shout, "YOU'RE OUT!" I was safe! I scored!

"Did you win?" someone asked.

Every year I still cut grass with a push power-mower, do the yardwork, and trimming. When I'm finished the yard shows its appreciation. I like dogs and cats. I like to watch the squirrels and birds chase each other. I like to look at cloud formations in the sky and wonder about things.

I haven't found answers to all of my questions – the "why" of things.

But, I persevere.

"Did you win?" again, someone asked.

"I think I did," I answered.

I hope to keep it this way.

I hope to keep it this way.

AFTERWARD

About 1930, one of the Henry families that lived at the southern tip of Ohio near Portsmouth moved north to Akron, Ohio, "The rubber capitol of the world." The next migration saw one-half of the family move to Los Angeles, California, "The movie capitol of the world." The final moves were made during 1950 to1970 time period, after more than thirty years of residing in Akron.

The first family member to leave and head west in late 1954 was Lyle Gordon Henry, the youngest of the Henry children. At nearly 18 years of age he decided to make a major change and move to Los Angeles. Robert Norman Henry, "the entertainer," made the move in 1955. He struck out for Hollywood after being involved and performing in show business. Bob passed away in 2010 having achieved his dream of living and working in Hollywood.

The oldest sibling, Willard Armand Henry and family relocated to the Los Angeles area in the early to mid-1960s. Willard died in the Los Angeles area in 1984.

Grandma and Grandpa Henry visited their sons in the Los Angeles area several times, spending a couple of months at a time. They became the last to leave Akron about 1970 while in their seventies. Arthur and Maggie joined their sons and established themselves in California. The Henry parents, Arthur and Maggie, passed away at 82 and 84 years of age, respectively, in California.

Maxine Lena Henry, George Raymond Henry, and Arthur Vernon Henry remained in Akron with their children's families nearby, until they passed away. Maxine lived the longest, at 96 years, and was the sole survivor of the original Henrys of Akron, until her death in 2019.

Lyle, at 87, is the last of the first Henrys in Akron. He was born in Akron and was named by his older brother, Vernon. Lyle is living in Bullhead City, Arizona, with his wife, Alita, after residing in Los Angeles for a number of years. He has two daughters and two sons.

Of the remaining second generation of Henrys born to Eva and Arthur Vernon Henry – Bob and Nancy still live in Akron. Don lives in Springboro, Ohio, and Patricia lives in Ft. Lauderdale, Florida.

What is there to learn from this close look into the Henry family since 1891, who have lived through the country's two world wars, a depression, an on-going cold war, a police action in Korea, race riots, men landing on the moon, Viet Nam, a roller-coaster economy, and assorted military campaigns in the Mid-East and elsewhere?

The take-away is Perseverance – like most families. It's about searching for and finding opportunities, adjusting when misfortune pops-up, and keeping your head above water financially. It's all about Mom and Dad, until you become mom and dad. Then, at times, the going may get tough, rough, and dire, but you must perform - you must persevere and forge on.

CONCLUSION

My life has been an "inside the park" homerun, I believe. I've touched every base as I ran, not as fast as when I passed first base, but I've gotten where I wanted to be. I've done nearly everything I wanted to do. Only recently I looked into my families' history as never before. Some interesting things have been found; perseverance is one of them, among others.

Do you think it matters if you don't know anything about your bloodline? Many who think about it, wonder if they have something to be proud about. Some have been led to believe they have royalty or men and women of great accomplishment, somewhere in their family background. My family, "The Henrys of Akron," always hoped, or half-believed we could have been related to Patrick Henry of Virginia. He was the great patriot and firebrand who called people to action against England's control by articulating his well-known speech, "Give me liberty, or give me death."

Maybe one of our Henry relatives thought he would find out, somehow, if our bloodline carried some of Patrick's genes. It's true, some Henrys, like Patrick, were known to be high-strung with short tempers and fiery commentary, erupting only when they were challenged in some manner, or drink got the best of them. Many of us probably thought it was a long shot and settled into a non-educated frame of mind – which was less stressful than attempting any plan or research into the matter, and without the tools of DNA that are more easily accessible today. We were content to think Patrick may have been one of us. Besides that, why waste a perfectly good day, taking time away from living life before you get old and can't enjoy what you have?

As I became aware of our family and relatives' situations it dawned on me at an early age that we were not well-off. We didn't have hot and cold running water and all the other basic things needed for a normal household. We didn't have television or social media to watch and explain how well-heeled people spend their time and their money as most kids are exposed to today. But, down deep I knew – I think we all knew – something was wrong with us. Our families could never get ahead or even consider reaching for the gold ring to change the course   of our lives. Money and other barriers lobbied against it. I don't know of any who dared to go against the conventions we found ourselves buried in, although every one of the Henrys probably had hopes that something or someone would come along and would help us climb out.

Out of all of our relatives and friends we were exposed to, only a couple of Henrys worked at self-determination, and who also pursued the American Dream with full commitment of body and mind. One of them was my dad, and the other was my mom. They did their very best to provide and nurture their children. In spite of their seventh and ninth grade educations, they forged-on doing their best to help us understand several virtues: you must work to get what you want; no one is better than anyone else; education is necessary; you must obey laws; and alcohol has no place in our lives – avoid it at all costs. With these dictums, we were sent to school every day to find our place in the world.

Over time, I began to mentally identify who had the makings of being smart, hardworking, and kind versus those who were lazy and less good as people. I don't remember the list, but my mom and dad stood out. More than anything else, they motivated my need to do something with my life that would result in a positive outcome. How was I going to do that? The answer was easy – do what's right. I learned by doing. I watched and observed the negative outcomes from drinking, avoiding work and being plain lazy. There were plenty of examples to go around. Instead, avoid alcohol and get busy working to overcome whatever obstacle there is, and that includes avoiding the wrong types of people.

Fear of failure always began with shaky knees and sometimes, shortness of breath, like I experienced in my early pursuit of money. Selling sachets, knocking on doors for the first time selling doughnuts, shining shoes in front of a beer joint, or becoming a paper boy on my first dark wintery night wading through the snow-filled sidewalks of the strange streets in Niles, Ohio, getting lost on the route and finding my way back. I sat down on a fireplug, angry and shivering, and ate a pack of cookies wondering, "What was this?"

As I got older and into heavier B-squad work assignments in Goodyear's tire plants, each work assignment was different from the day before. Sometimes I worked a double shift with no extra lunch and no sleep because of school, then back again another night, another new job, more stress trying to keep up with "piece-work" production rates, and then moving on to a full-time salaried job in Goodyear's Research and Development lab. My knees shook, standing for the first time in front of a massive Consolidated 21-101 Mass Spectrometer and learning how to operate the monster – it caused my nerves to quiver, but not my motivation and not my goal. They were intact. I wanted to be free from financial insecurity. I wanted to achieve, I wanted to never have to say, I've failed.

But, I did. I failed. I succumbed when I reached a point where I felt I had achieved what was wanted most – a loving, smart and optimistic wife, two happy and healthy blonde-haired boys, a new brick house, and continuing to pursue a college degree.

I looked around one day and decided school wasn't needed. All I had to do was work at Goodyear's R&D lab and that was it – I had it made. Maybe I got lazy.

The Consolidated 21-101's red and green button lights were blinking. So was I. I blinked, and woke up to the fact that there had to be something else I could do. Mentally, I doubled back and touched second base again, to be certain I was on the right path.

I had no demons to exorcise, no psychological problems to assuage, I wanted to do something that made me feel I was accomplishing something, achieving something useful, and to use my life to the best of my abilities. I thought about the Salvation Army where I had spent time during grammar school and teenage years. It plagued me until I took action. My wife totally understood. However difficult it was for her to make this crazy turn-about palatable, she made the decision to join me through the upsetting change. It wasn't an easy thing. We sold the house, moved to New York City in the Bronx and entered Officer Training School.

Well, by this time you would have read how things turned out. And, if that wasn't the craziest thing I've done, I turned around and did it again. After receiving a Master's degree four years later, I left my job at Goodyear Aerospace as an administrative engineer to take charge of a Salvation Army Corps in Sandusky, Ohio, with the intent of finishing our Training School requirements and becoming full-time officers in 1969. Was this crazy, or what? I should have been legally incarcerated in a mental facility, with Marilyn holding the key. Some would think this couldn't be justified, but I had to get it out of my system.

I leave the rest of my story up to you. I could continue, but I'm going to "slip back into the hospital bed of my mind and clam up," for I fear I am talking too much.

So, what about you? What is your story, the "who, what, why, and when" of your hard working existence, or maybe and hopefully, your wonderful life. Have you achieved your dream, or your goals to your own satisfaction, and have you given any thought or wondered about your ancestors, and your family that, historically, made you the way you are, today?

Now, back to my story – one of the more interesting facts to come out of my search was information my first cousin on my paternal side, Matt Dexter, a top notch genealogy and DNA researcher who advised me. It concerned my Grandma Henry (Norris). I don't think anyone knew about it. Legally she was a Norris; DNA-wise no she wasn't, she was an Atwell. Her second Great Grandfather Norris was adopted, therefore, I am not a Norris either. I'm an Atwell. What a surprise. I researched the Atwells back to 1530, and found no kings or queens.

As the story closes, I finished my running slide into home plate. The ball whizzed by my shoulder – the catcher leaped over me, with yellow dust cascading and bellowing in the air over the two scrambling bodies – and the ball careened off of his protective mask, out of reach.

The Umpire straightened up his hunched-over back. He remained silent, didn't stick his thumb into the air. He crossed and waved his arms. He shouted, "SAFE." I was safe! I scored!

"Did you win?" someone asked.

"I think I did."

I hope to keep it this way.

THE TREK

The Earliest Settlers

Ireland

John Henry of Ireland, 1710 – 1790, is the focal point of the Henry immigration to America. In 1745 John was 35 years of age and his wife, Dorothy Ryder, was 20 when they became parents of John Henry, Sr. The son was born in Antrim, Ireland in 1745 on the northeast part of the country. No one knew their son's destination would be to settle in America.

John Sr. arrived in Mason, Mason County Virginia sometime before 1769 when his wife, Margaret Pilson (1750-1828) gave birth to John Henry, Jr. before the Revolutionary War broke out. Another son, Samuel Lemuel Henry, was born after the war in 1789 in Patrick, Virginia. Samuel and Sarah Henry (Lee) had thirteen children, one of whom, Daniel Henry, would be the ancestor of an Ohio family that had moved from Ironton, Ohio, to Akron, Ohio, around 1928. The family consisted of parents Arthur Vinton Henry and Margaret Ann Norris; their children Willard, Vernon, George, Maxine, and later born in Akron – Robert and Lyle.

England

Thomas Edward Norris, Sr. was born on October 16, in Congham, Norfolk, England. He was the son of Geoffrey Norris and Anne Mary Norris. At eleven years of age he ran away from home to become a cabin boy, a sailor, and a trader. He landed in Nansemond county, Virginia colony in 1630 and decided to stay. He married Ann Hynson in 1637. Thomas was busy, a businessman, trader, and planter, and had many dealings in a variety of pursuits. During these times and early American periods, a family consisted of many sons and daughters. There is a book about him written by Pearl Mitchell Mallory, "Thomas Norris – The Immigrant." The first person with the surname, Norris, in the province of Virginia was Thomas Norris, Sr., who had been a cabin boy, born in England and who had later died in Talbot County, Maryland colony.

The Trek

The migration of the Henry families/Norris families continued through the American Revolution and Civil War, moving west into West Virginia, Kentucky, and Ohio. Many of the Henry and Norris families built lives in a small area of southern Ohio, near Portsmouth, Ohio, Scioto County, and a city named Ironton, Ohio, in Lawrence County. There were industries located along the Ohio River, including coal mining, ceramic manufacturing, railroad, steel making, and furnace services. There is a place in Ironton where many Henry families will remain; a place that their forbearers located; it's quiet and peaceful, a place dedicated to the Henry name, it's called the Henry Cemetery. It can be located by searching www.findagrave .com/cemetery/1075038/henry-cemetery.

Finally, I couldn't find any connection between the Henry surname and Patrick Henry, the great patriot and signer of the Declaration of Independence. The only connection is this

– Samuel Henry was born in Patrick County, Virginia, adjacent to Henry County, both counties were named after Patrick Henry.

Through the Revolutionary War, The Civil War, and the pioneer living conditions, the Henrys worked and lived, married and died, with a branch of the tree moving from Ironton, Ohio, to Akron, Ohio, to find new adventures and new opportunities in the rubber capital of the world, because of Arthur and Maggie Henry (Norris).

THE GENTHOLTZS AND ERWINS OF AKRON, OHIO

Germany

John Gentholtz was born in 1816 in an area of Germany known as Baden-Wurtenberg, bordering France and Switzerland. Somehow he traveled to America, but it's unknown how and when he made the trip. At some point he settled in Niles, Ohio, with his wife, Susannah Loveland in 1849.

Charles and Deborah Gentholtz's locations are unknown prior to residing in Akron, Ohio. Niles is a good guess for both. If both parent's names aren't available on web sites, they are difficult to find, unless in-depth research is undertaken. At least some basic facts are found on web sites in most genealogies for those who are searching.

In addition, some facts may be in error or simply left unknown, reasons for which no one will know. For example, Nettie Matilda Erwin (Gentholtz) is recorded as having a daughter, Lilian Fedelia Erwin (1913-1915) her first born, whom no one presently is aware had existed with the passage of time. Similarly, Nettie's children line-up shows Esther Marie Erwin, but not Eva Lena Erwin. Esther and Eva were born as twins, actually triplets, but the third girl, Edith, died at birth. And to further frustrate searchers and to complicate things, another daughter, Daisy Erwin, the oldest daughter isn't recorded either.

Thomas Erwin's genealogy isn't traced to the country of origin, which we believe is Scotland, due to lack of information beyond Alexander Erwin, 1820 -1889. Further research could lead to Ireland or Germany. Most known Erwin family movement was between Niles and Akron in Ohio, and Wheatland, Sharon and Oil City, in Pennsylvania.

Henry Family Tree

John Henry	1710 –
Dorothy Ryder (or Rider)	1725 – 1781
Antrim, Antrim Ireland	

John Henry, Sr.	1745 – 1818
Margaret Pilson	1750 - 1828

Samuel Lemuel Henry	1792 – 1845
Sarah Henry (Lee)	1793 – 1885

Daniel Henry	1816 – 1880
Hester Ann Henry (Queen)	1818 -

Daniel was difficult to validate. His birth was in Patrick, Virgina, then later moved to Lawrence County, Ohio, where he worked as a furnace laborer. Hester's genealogy traced to Archibold McQueen (1671 – 1754) and Florence McQueen (MacDonald) 1698 –1791. They lived in Inverness, Scotland.

John William Henry	1844 – 1917
Mary Ellen Henry (Coon)	1846 – 1918

William Vinton Henry	1862 – 1909
Mary A. Henry (Ervin) *	1870 – 1941

Arthur Vinton Henry	1891 - 1973

Thomas Edward Norris, Sr.	1608 – 1678
Ann Norris (Hynson)	
Congham, Norfolk England	

John Norris, Sr.	1643 – 1710
Susannah Norris (Heard)	1656 – 1719

John Norris, Jr.	1680 – 1760
Ann Norris (Wheatley)	1702 – 1775

John Norris	1722 – 1780
Jane Norris (Stevenson)	1720 – 1788

William Norris	1745 – 1775
Sarah Norris (Claiborne)	1744 – 1824

John Claiborne Norris	1775 – 1847
Nancy Norris (Morgan)	1775 – 1800

John Wesley Norris	1796 – 1877
Margaret Polly Norris (Songer)	1804 – 1842

John David Norris	1824 – 1878
Sarah Norris (Broom)	1824 – 1898

John William Norris	1844 – 1917
Julia Ann Norris (Dean)	1844 – 1927

George Willard Norris	1865 – 1931
Alma Norris (Sanders)	1873 – 1950

Maggie Ann Henry (Norris)	1896 – 1979

Arthur Vernon Henry	7/20/1919 – 2/12/1977

*Mary Henry for familysearch.org - Mary A Ervin for geni.com

Don Henry

Rev. 4/9/2022

Erwin Family Tree

John Gentholtz 1816 – 1892 Susannah Gentholtz (Loveland) 1825 – 1899 John was born in Germany, area of Baden-Wurtenberg bordering Switzerland and France. John immigrated to the U.S. and settled in Niles, Ohio.	Alexander Erwin 1820 -1889 Eliiza Erwin (Weiss) 1821 - Alexander, a wagon maker, and Eliza were married in 1840 and lived in Mineral Ridge, Niles, Ohio, Trumbull County.
Charles James Gentholtz 1866 - 1947 Deborah Hepsebeth Gentholtz 1862 - 1919	Nelson Erwin 1845 – 1890 Hannah Erwin (Brown) 1850 -
Nettie Matilda Erwin (Gentholtz) 1887 – 1961 Nettie became blind in early childhood, but it never affected her ability to learn and to be an effective home maker and mother.	Thomas Albert Erwin 1882 – 1949 Tom served in World War I, and brought home some of his equipment, a helmet, a gas mask, and bayonet.

Eva Lena Henry (Erwin) 3/22/ 1921 – 10/12/1987

Don Henry

Mar 14, 2022